This book is dedicated to the Muse,
in whatever form She appears, and to you, the reader,
the magical creative who is critical to the beauty and
enchantment in the world.

Paula Chaffee Scardamalia

ENCHANTING CREATIVITY

How Fairy Tales, Dreams, Rituals & Journaling Can Awaken Your Creative Self

REDFeather™

MIND | BODY | SPIRIT

4880 Lower Valley Road, Atglen, PA 19310

Other REDFeather Titles by the Author:
Tarot for the Fiction Writer: How 78 Cards Can Take You from Idea to Publication, Paula Scardamalia, ISBN 978-0-7643-5723-7

Other REDFeather Titles on Related Subjects:
The Teaching Power of Dreams, Brad and Sherry Steiger, ISBN 978-0-924608-04-9
The Muse in You, Lynn Newman, ISBN 978-0-7643-5717-6
The Creativity Oracle, Amy Zerner, ISBN 978-0-7643-5899-9

Designed by Brenda McCallum
Cover design by Ashley Millhouse

ISBN: 978-0-7643-6375-7
Printed in India

Published by REDFeather Mind, Body, Spirit
An imprint of Schiffer Publishing, Ltd.
4880 Lower Valley Road
Atglen, PA 19310
Phone: (610) 593-1777; Fax: (610) 593-2002
Email: Info@redfeathermbs.com
Web: www.redfeathermbs.com

For our complete selection of fine books on this and related subjects, please visit our website at www.redfeathermbs.com. You may also write for a free catalog.

REDFeather Mind, Body, Spirit's titles are available at special discounts for bulk purchases for sales promotions or premiums. Special editions, including personalized covers, corporate imprints, and excerpts, can be created in large quantities for special needs. For more information, contact the publisher.

We are always looking for people to write books on new and related subjects. If you have an idea for a book, please contact us at proposals@schifferbooks.com.

CONTENTS

ACKNOWLEDGMENTS

The journey of this book began in 2000, when I first pitched it at the Maui Writers Conference, so thank you, Sam Horn, for stepping into my craft booth in Virginia and urging me to become part of the conference as a speaker host. I didn't see the wings and magic wand at first, so I didn't realize I was in the presence of a fairy godmother.

Thank you to another fairy godmother, Zita Christian, who is not only a sister writer enchanted by story, but a celebrant who has taught me most of what I know about ritual . . . and magic.

Barbara Biziou was my first exposure to ritual outside the church, teaching the joy of shaping your own personal rituals and blessings. Many thanks for that workshop at Skidmore all those years ago.

Many of my early opportunities to teach aspects of this work came through the International Women's Writing Guild (IWWG), an amazing and unique writers organization. If you are a woman writer, please do yourself a favor and check them out at iwwg.org.

Once again, Ciro Marchetti's art adorns my book, and I am so grateful for his generous spirit and his dedication, his "I do," to his creativity. His Tarot decks, puzzles, and other artwork have brightened my life, that of my clients, and the viewers of my Monday Tarot Message from the Muse on social media.

Thanks again to Schiffer Publishing for the opportunity to share this creative journey, especially Christopher R. McClure, Peggy Kellar, and Brenda McCallum for understanding the enchantment of fairy tale and creativity.

This book was written during a world pandemic, and I am grateful to the sister writers of the Saturday Writing Retreat for connection and creative support—Misty, Rona, Delia, and especially Win, who, in addition to being part of the retreat group, is also a dear friend and accountability partner. Hearing her voice five days a week helped me breathe through the labor pains of this book. And she was patient with my whining.

Part of my understanding of the creative journey comes through watching my three sons grow and progress with their own creative work. Stephen and his wife, Mindy, work creative magic with their two sons every day. Stephen's photography captures the magic of nature so you see a glimpse of nature's mysteries. Christopher uses his brilliance as a wordsmith to inform and convince and connect. His passion for and commitment to his work seldom wanes. Jason, with his music and photography, is willing to pursue his Muse wherever She leads, through the forest, to the top of mountains, in the recording studio, and beyond. No hedge will get in his way. I am so proud of them all.

There are no words to express the deep gratefulness for having a creative partner that values and supports my work. The man in my life, a.k.a. dear hubby Bob, shows his creativity in everything he does, from his own teaching and consulting, to restoring his MGs, to building shelves for his grandsons. He's a creative gift that keeps on giving, and I'm grateful for him every day.

PART ONE

CREATIVITY, DREAMS, AND
FAIRY TALES

Introduction

I am a queen in Egypt, and it is time for me to go to the temple. I exit through the back door of my house, similar to my grandfather's in waking reality. My hair brushes my chin as I move gracefully, regally, in my long dress. Two men servants, dressed only in black loincloths, hurry forward and stoop with their backs to me so that I may climb on their shoulders and be carried. Their backs and shoulders are muscled and tan, their heads bald. I climb up onto the shoulders of the one on the right. He lifts me and walks toward the temple that sits on a rise of sand off to the left. The sun is bright and hot.

The manservant compliments my dress, which is long and straight and has a soft loopy texture in browns and turquoise. I thank him, and he sets me gently down at the steps of the temple. Four more servants in white loincloths with white headdresses rush forward with a sedan chair. I walk toward it, knowing my subjects wait for me inside the temple. I straighten, almost grow taller with power and the energy running through my veins. My chamberlain and other servants wait at the top of the temple steps to escort me inside.

As I sit down in the sedan chair, a man, one of my subjects, emerges from the temple and stands in the doorway, unrolling a long scroll of colored silk about 8 inches wide. In a loud voice, he reads a list of complaints, demanding redress of wrongs. After he finishes, he turns to go back inside. I nod at one of my administrators, bearded and in the long garment of aristocracy, who is sitting next to the door. I want the subject to be retained so I may question him later, but the administrator stabs him with a knife!

I am horrified! I did not want him killed!

Have you ever had a dream like this, from another time and place, that startled you awake?

I had this dream when I was thirty-two, happily married, and the mother of three young sons. We lived in an old farmhouse heated ineffectively with a woodstove. Four months before the dream, my mother, fifty-three, died of breast cancer. I still grieved, and, as part of my grieving process, I kept a journal of both my waking and dreaming life.

My mother and I were the best of friends, sharing interests in art and books and, of course, raising children. Her death not only ripped at my heart but ripped open the door into my dream life. Even though I'd been an active dreamer since childhood, because of several significant dreams before and after her death I paid more attention to my dreams. I recorded them, while also reading numerous books about dreams and dreaming.

Then, I had the Egyptian Queen dream. What was that about? What was going on here?

At that time, I was reading Gayle Delaney's book *Living Your Dreams*. Using her method of working with dreams, I concluded that my temple dream was about the sacredness of my creativity. My creative temple was filled with my subjects, the ideas and projects, waiting for my arrival and attention, and the horrifying stabbing was the sabotage of my creativity. I was stabbing my creativity in the back.

Because of its clarity and power, I couldn't ignore the message. Diligently, I made time to write, edit, and polish a young-adult fantasy written several years before. In spite of a house that was barely warm, and three little boys continually sick with flu and other childhood illnesses, I sat down at the computer and worked. The image of that dream, of killing my creativity, haunted me and compelled me to keep at it. I also continued to weave.

Six months later, I had another significant dream.

I am at a local gallery, admiring a weaving supposedly created by someone else.

"Who wove it?" I asked.

"Paula," the gallery director answered.

My name! I looked at the clear image of the weaving, a floating landscape in soft blues and violets.

In a few months, the dream image and a variation were woven and off my loom.

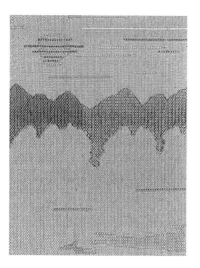

I titled them *Transcendence I* and *Transcendence II*. Several months later, that image was chosen as the cover design by a professor at the state university whose book title was *Mediated Transcendence*.

In the early '90s, I registered for a workshop on dreams held at a local New Age shop. The instructor, Robert Moss, taught the shamanic approach to working with and understanding dreams. I took many classes, went on dream retreats he led, and was a member of his dream circle for years. Soon, not only was I working with my dreams, I taught dreamwork to others and helped them understand their dreams. My favorite attendees and clients were writers and creatives.

Where then does the story of Sleeping Beauty enter the picture—or the dreams?

That fairy tale fascinated me from the time I was a little girl. Maybe it was the spell of sleep, the hedge of thorns, or, because I've always been a romantic, the magic power of a kiss. I've loved and been fascinated by that fairy tale for most of my life, especially by the ideas of sleeping for generations and a castle hidden by a hedge of thorns.

But the first time it became more than a tale and became a waking dream was when I was a young mother. I was rocking our third son, still an infant, to sleep for the night. As I rocked back and forth, back and forth, in the dark silence of the room, where the only sound was the slight creak of the rocker and the soft breath of my son, who was nestled into my shoulder, I had a vision, a sense of the Prince walking into Sleeping Beauty's castle, where everyone was asleep.

What must it have been like to open the heavy door into an enchanted space where everyone and everything, even the fire, slept? Was he afraid to break the silence? Why would anyone wish to cross that threshold?

Feeling the beating heart of my infant son against my chest, I imagined the beating heart of the prince, loud in the silence, his own indrawn breath a rasping noise against the noiseless texture of the castle. I sensed his desire to find the Princess weighted with trepidation. Who did he think he was?

While I continued to rock with the image, I realized I did not like the idea of a beautiful young woman lying passively and still as death for generations while waiting for her prince to come. It didn't feel right. What was her story?

Years after I had the dream, after attending Moss's classes, and through my own reading and research into dreams, myths, and fairy tales, I decided that Sleeping Beauty was experiencing her own initiation into womanhood. And she was doing it in the dreamtime.

Understanding her role in the tale also helped me reach a new understanding of the Prince's role in the tale as a complement to hers, not as rescuer but as awakener, as the one who recalls her to life and the community. Then, it wasn't a stretch to view the fairy tale as a rich metaphor for the creative process. The story models the way that both the intuitive, receptive, dreaming aspects of creativity combine with the practical, active, community-oriented aspects to transform idea into reality, and concept into product, and to make wishes, desires, and dreams into something we can touch, hold, see, smell, and hear.

Like dreams, fairy tales and myths have many layers of understanding and meaning. These are discovered, rediscovered, and seen anew as times and cultural attitudes and beliefs change. This fairy tale, this story, as all good stories, is both personal and universal.

In this book, you'll learn how to remember, record, and work with the Muse's dream messages, which shout you awake at night or whisper so softly in your ear that you almost don't remember them.

You'll learn how to keep a dream journal so you can easily refer back to those Muse messages again and again, as well as receive journal prompts that you can use to understand your creative process and spark new ways of working with your Muse.

Since we all use rituals, whether we are conscious of it or not, you'll discover how to design rituals that fuel and support your creative life.

And integrating these tools with your creative process is the fairy tale, along with its siblings and cousins, so that you have a magical tale to help you brave the thorns and curses encountered in your creative life, and to live your happily ever after.

MAGIC, METAPHOR, AND METAMORPHOSIS

Metamorphosis defines the fairy tale. —Marina Warner

Metamorphosis, according to Merriam-Webster, is "a change of physical form or substance especially by supernatural means." Other definitions state that the change is caused by natural or supernatural means.

The idea of the supernatural also participates in the definition of magic. According to Merriam-Webster, magic is "the use of means (such as charms or spells) believed to have supernatural power over natural forces . . . an extraordinary power or influence seemingly from a supernatural source . . . something that seems to cast a spell: enchantment."

What makes me smile about this definition of magic is that many times, customers in my weaving booth at craft shows, people reading my newsletter or books, and even other creatives often talk about the magic of creativity. To others, it often appears that creatives practice magic and metamorphosis. Transform one thing into another. Change a group of notes into a tune and into an emotion. A lump of clay into a pot. Threads into fabric or garment. Ingredients into a gourmet meal. Creativity is all about metamorphosis and transformation. Magic.

In the well-known oracle deck the Tarot, the Magician of the Major Arcana often stands with a finger pointing to the sky, and a finger of the other hand pointing to the earth. As Rachel Pollack says in her book *Tarot Wisdom*, "This posture often makes the card attractive to artists, healers, and other people who work with manifesting energy. Almost all creative people will say that when the work is going well . . . they are simply the channel to bring the work into the physical world." To others, they appear to be working magic.

Both metamorphosis and magic share the principles of change and apparent supernatural forces. Those principles are also present in our oldest stories: myth and fairy tale.

How many myths or fairy tales can you think of where a person, animal, or object changes from one thing into another?

Think of Pygmalion and his statue turned woman. Cinderella's pumpkin coach and her rat footmen. The frog who turns into a prince once kissed. Zeus, who turned into swan or bull. Those are a few that come to my mind. What about you?

One Christmas when I was a preteen, my siblings and I received a gift from our maternal aunt, *The Big Golden Book of Fairy Tales*. In that collection of tales from Europe and Asia was the story of the seven (sometimes twelve) swans. In it, the mother of seven brothers and one sister dies. The father remarries. The new stepmother, for one reason or another, casts a spell on the seven brothers, turning them into swans, who resume their human form only at night. Their sister is left to mourn their loss until she discovers that to break the spell, she must gather stinging nettles, break them down, and spin the fibers into a yarn that she must then knit into a sweater for each of her brothers. And if that isn't enough to test a person, she must do all this under a vow of silence, knitting them each a sweater made from a green yarn spun from stinging nettles.

While setting about her mission, she is tested, but her biggest challenge arises when she is put on trial for witchcraft because she spends too much time in the graveyard—her source of nettles, which, of course, she can't explain. Vow of silence, remember? All she can do is keep knitting, even as they stack the wood around her feet and light the pyre. As the flames flare up, out of the sky fly the seven swans, her brothers. As they pass her, she throws a sweater on each, breaking the spell and returning them to human form. All except the last brother, whose sweater was missing a sleeve because she didn't have time or materials to finish it. He is human except for one wing.

Transformation. Metamorphosis. Shape-shifting. Through the magical power of knitting, craft, creativity. The blending of those ideas was so powerful for me that decades later, I named my weaving business Nettles and Green Threads. And my love of fairy tales and myths led to the design of a workshop for writers titled "Myths, Fairy Tales, and Archetypes for Story."

But what exactly is a fairy tale? Why is it important for you as a creative?

Marina Warner, author of *From the Beast to the Blonde* and *Once Upon a Time*, writes of a fairy tale having several characteristics that separate it from other forms of story.

Among those characteristics, several are important for our purposes.

One is that fairy tales were not associated with the literate elite but with the *volk*, the common folk. You didn't have to be able to read to share one of the tales, or to be able to enjoy it. Until many of the tales were gathered into collections such as those of the Grimm brothers or Charles Perrault, fairy tales were part of an oral tradition. This association with the common folk is a reminder to you that creativity exists in many forms and is not the purview of the elite. Your creative work does not have to be labeled classical or fine art or literature in order for it to have a significance in the lives of others.

Let me repeat that, because it's easy for creatives to forget. Your work does not have to be labeled classical or fine art or literature in order for it to have a significance in the lives of others.

Which is not to say that the tales or your work won't and don't cross over into those realms, just that it need not.

Another important characteristic is that, as Warner writes, "fairy tale consists above all of acts of imagination." Acts of imagination. Sound familiar? Isn't that what creativity is in all its many and various forms—acts of imagination?

Yet another defining characteristic of the fairy tale is the element of wonder. In fact, according to Warner, an alternative term for fairy tale is "wonder tale." The supernatural elements and suspension of natural physical laws generate a magical reality that leads to a state of wonder. As I mentioned earlier in this chapter, if you've ever sold your work at a craft show or art exhibit or stayed after a performance to hear the audience's comments, then you know that it's not unusual to hear, "How did you do that? Where did you get the ability (or idea or talent)? That was *wonderful*! I could never do that." For them, you just suspended natural laws and gave them an experience of something beyond their worlds.

Did you see the film *Billy Elliot*, released in 2000? It's a story about a coal miner's son who wants to dance. Against prejudices, family expectations, and more, Billy succeeds in following his dream. In the closing scene of the film, he is dancing in Matthew Bourne's *Swan Lake*. And he leaps onto the stage in a way that appears as if he is flying, as if he just suspended natural laws and gave the audience, including his father and others, an experience of something beyond their worlds. That is the power of creative magic, your creative magic.

Where creativity might diverge from fairy tale is in fairy tale's usual expression of hope, that "happily ever after" that we look for in those tales. You know that whether we talk about creative process or a creative project, neither one necessarily promises a happily ever after in the way that fairy tale does. This is not to say that there aren't trials and dangers and monsters and sacrifices and death in fairy tales, but rather that, at the end of the tales, there is a promise that those things need not prevail.

It would be nice to have a magic wand to wave when a project or process isn't going the way you want it to. I hope the tools here help, because if I could wave a magic wand, I would give every creative and every creative project a happily-ever-after ending. But that is not within my power. It is within your power.

The first tool on the journey is one that artists and creatives have used for centuries to record their experiences and track their progress, the journal.

JOURNALS FOR DREAMING
AND CREATING

The practice of keeping a journal has come in and out of my life and has changed appearances several times. Because friends know I love journals, I have a stack of blank journals as well as a file drawer and a shelf of filled journals. I've filled notebooks with Morning Pages, a creative practice from Julia Cameron's *The Artist's Way*, with the ideas and frustrations of being an entrepreneur, with letters to my mother after she died, with sleep and conscious dreams, and with the hopes and dreams of a writer and weaver searching for success.

In my book *Weaving a Woman's Life: Spiritual Lessons from the Loom*, I write that a journal, not diamonds, is a girl's best friend. It can be a guy's best friend as well. A journal is a record keeper, a secret holder, and a place to explore the inner world, especially the inner creative world.

The idea of keeping a journal used to carry with it the responsibility of writing daily in it. One more thing on the to-do list. But the journal is a tool that is supposed to serve you, not you it. Any suggestions about keeping journals that I offer here are only ideas and possibilities for you to try.

As I mentioned, I've kept all kinds of journals for all kinds of reasons, but two that I fall back on again and again and that serve the purpose of this book are the creative project journal and the dream journal. As a writer, if I am working on a novel, I like to have a project journal where I keep notes about characters, settings, themes, conflicts, and even the spreads of the Tarot cards I pull for that writing session. For projects like this book, I'll keep a journal filled with references to articles and books, quotes, chapter ideas or thoughts, even images. My mother, who was a watercolor artist, kept sketchbooks, journals filled with drawings, watercolor sketches or studies, color schemes, and even notes.

How you keep your creative journal often depends on your creative medium, but even if you are a writer, a journal is a good place to draw, collage, and adhere photos, postcards, dried flowers, and mementos. Whatever stirs and keeps stirring those creative juices.

You don't have to write or record in complete sentences or thoughts. Lists, bullet points, and mind mapping are effective journaling techniques. Nor do you have to censor yourself, because your journal is for you. Whatever you record there is not a measure of your creativity or your skills. It's a place for your musings and conversations with your Muse.

You can find journals online and in bookstores and specialty shops. I've listed several journal makers that I use and like. And that's one necessary requirement, that you like and feel comfortable with a journal. I usually like ones with soft covers so that I can fold them back and work with only one side of the journal.

Another important element of keeping a journal is a comfortable, pleasing-to-use writing instrument, or sketching or drawing tools. Believe it or not, I love using fountain pens and now have a collection of them that I've bought or been given. My friend Rachel Pollack uses them for all her writing, and she got me hooked.

But you might use pastels or charcoal or mechanical pencils. Whatever rocks your creative boat and keeps you engaged in the process.

The other type of journal for your creativity is a dream journal. This journal is where you record dreams, both sleeping and conscious dreams. The reason for the separate dream journal is because once you start paying attention to them, you'll find you more frequently remember your dreams and will fill pages with them. Plus, one of the uses of a dream journal besides recording your dreams is the development of your own dream dictionary, the best dream dictionary you'll ever have.

Also, in a dream journal, you keep a table of contents where you record the title, the date, and the page number of a dream, so you can easily refer back to it when you wish.

How to keep a dream journal will be shared in a later chapter. For now, know that journals are an important tool for your creative life. And however you use them, they will help you before, during, and after your once upon a time.

Journal Work

If you don't already have some blank journals at hand, use the resources at the back of this book to go shopping online for a journal that you might enjoy keeping. Or, if you can, make a visit to a bookstore so that you can actually feel the journal, turn its pages, and discover if the two of you can have a working relationship. Do the same for a writing tool.

Then write in your journal how you listen for and pay attention to your Muse. Do you record what you hear? How? Would you like to do anything differently?

ONCE UPON A TIME

Once upon a time . . .

That phrase, "Once upon a time . . . ," is a promise.

A promise that the story that follows holds certain elements: a sense of timelessness or a time long ago, magical creatures such as talking animals and vegetables that change into other things such as a carriage, and, of course, a happily-ever-after ending. It's a time and place where almost anything can and does happen.

"Once upon a time" signals to the listener that it is time to settle down, get quiet, and prepare to listen. Imagine a storyteller of long ago, sitting in a circle of folk around a fire, or surrounded by women stitching or spinning or knitting while wee ones played at their feet. The storyteller clears their throat and speaks those four attention-grabbing words. The chatter and laughter stops. Quiet falls except for the crackle of the fire or the whir of a spinning wheel.

Now. Now they are prepared to listen to the story that follows, a story that may seem impossible and fantastical but in which they are willing to be part of merely by listening.

When you want to communicate with or hear your Muse, you have to give them—and yourself—a signal and time to prepare to listen before you actually begin the work. You need a signal to settle down, get quiet, and listen, not just to the original inspirational idea but to the ongoing conversation that the Muse or your creative project wants to have with you.

"Once upon a time" is a well-known, ancient signal for storytellers and their listeners, dating from 1380 according to the Oxford English Dictionary, but there are other folkloric and fairy-tale signals as well. Often, the tales begin simply with "Once . . . ," such as "Once, there was a king, who . . ." That signal traverses cultures from Western to Eastern, and beyond. Other phrases serve as signals in other places, such as Nigeria or Chile, but the purpose remains the same—to grab attention and set up expectations for what is to follow.

As a creative, only you know what signal grabs your attention and prepares you for what follows. That is, what you are most likely to respond to so that you are ready to focus on and listen to the idea, the tale your Muse wants to spin for you, and the project.

Is it a phrase or sentence overheard in a conversation? The way the sunlight hits the dew on a raspberry? Is it a thrush singing at sunset? Or is it an inner restlessness that won't be still until you are? Or is it a dream?

Something captures your attention. Then the challenge is whether or not you will listen long enough to fully receive the inspiration or guidance.

Years ago—or, once upon a time, if you will—when I was a young mother with three boys underfoot in a yet-to-be-restored farmhouse, I was washing dishes (no dishwasher) and suddenly had an idea for a story. It captured my attention. Did I stop washing the dishes to capture this marvelous idea? Sadly, no. I kept washing dishes, and when I was done, as I watched the water drain from the sink, the idea swirled down the drain with the dishwater. How often has that happened to you? Maybe your signal, your idea didn't go down the drain with the dishwater, but, one way or another, it disappeared while you carried on doing the thing you were doing. You heard "Once upon a time . . . ," and, instead of getting quiet and listening, you kept on talking or watching television or scanning social media.

In today's constant noise of social media, work, family, television, and more, sometimes even when you want to, getting quiet in order to hear the tale your Muse wants to tell is challenging, often frustrating. Two things will help you pay attention and listen in such a way that you won't lose the thread of the tale or see it go down the drain.

First is practice. Just as you practice your art or craft, it's important to practice listening to the creative voice, the Muse, the signals. It's like training your ear in music. If you are a musician, then you probably know that an ear for music is developed through training and practice. That's why music schools require their students to take a class in ear training. A student's ear for music improves daily with even a small amount of practice each day.

This same understanding and practice is applicable to training you to listen for and to the signal preparing you for the fairy tale your Muse wants to tell you.

The practice can take many forms. Sitting somewhere and just listening, discerning what you hear and what may be missing. For example, I love sitting outside on our patio and listening. I hear birdsong, the water in our fountain, the air moving through the trees, a tree frog, a bee buzzing. What I don't hear is the rush of traffic or other people's voices. That absence might signal to some a quiet time of day, maybe early evening, when people have stopped moving around and interacting. Or it might signal, accurately, that I live in the country, and it is more normal to note the absence rather than the presence of those sounds.

If you are a visual artist, your "listening" might be sitting somewhere observing the mother pushing a stroller with two pairs of legs, the unexpected curl of leaves on an old tree, or the lace effect of waves washing up on a sandy beach. If you are a dancer, your listening might be imitating the swaying of willow branches in the breeze, or the leg movements of a heron fishing at the edge of a pond.

All of the "listening," though, is done without the sounds of computer, or phone, or television. Listening is done with presence and focus, even when you are working on your current project in your studio or office or favorite coffee shop.

Muse isn't just a noun; it's also a verb. The dictionary says that the verb "muse" means to ponder, reflect, meditate on (i.e., *to listen to the inner voice*). In addition to pondering and reflecting, musing (coming from the Old French, *muser*) can mean to stand with one's nose in the air as a dog does, to sniff the air, to catch the scent, the signal.

But to catch the scent in the first place, to have a trail to follow, you have to be willing to muse and ponder, to pay attention when you catch the scent. To muse with your Muse.

Whatever form your practice of listening takes, however you put your nose to the air to catch the signal, the second way to help you catch the signal and listen is to use the tools shared in this book—dreams, rituals, and journals.

The use of journals for catching the scent, for listening to the signal, and then working with the messages of the Muse is important, as evidenced by the history of journals for this purpose and the number of creatives who use them in one form or another.

Rituals are another tool that helps prepare you to hear the Muse's story, her insight, and her guidance. Like journals and the other tool, dreams, which will be shared in another chapter, rituals are an ancient tool, one that is effective for transitions, inspiration, and support.

Over the course of several centuries, the original meaning of some words in our living language changes, and the words lose their original impact and significance. *Ritual* and *routine* are two of those words that because of another word—repetition—are often used interchangeably and shouldn't be. Look at a current dictionary and you'll discover that both words have the idea of a repeated procedure as one of several meanings. But if you look at the origins of the words, you'll see how they differ.

MINDLESS ROUTINE

Routine comes from the French word, spelled the same way, meaning "usual course of action, beaten path," deriving from its root, *route*, meaning way, path, or course. In other words, a routine is a path or course of action that you repeat or travel over and over again. Routines make your life easier and more efficient because, after a period of time, you don't have to think about the order or steps of your actions anymore; you simply do them, saving time and brainpower.

For example, if every morning you had to think about whether or not to exercise first, then shower, then eat, or to eat before showering, time and energy would be wasted while trying to make this decision anew. Routines like this do not necessarily require any awareness other than that you are awake and functioning.

FORMAL RITUAL

Rituals, however, are more about *mindfulness* than *mindlessness*.

Barbara Biziou, in her book *The Joy of Ritual*, writes, "The word *ritual*, derived from an Indo-European root meaning 'to fit together,' conveys an act in which we literally join the metaphysical with the physical as a means of calling Spirit into our material lives."

Like the magician of the Tarot, that's what you do as a creative—call the metaphysical, the inspired idea, into the physical realm.

From the Latin word *ritualis*, relating to (religious) rites (from *ritus*, "rite"; religious observance or ceremony), the word "ritual" again conveys a set of actions having to do with the transcendent or sacred, such as you would find practiced in a church or other sacred space.

While current usage tends to reduce the word to the mundane equivalent of routine, as a creative you bring that sense of the sacred back to the word when you use rituals to add depth, focus, and awareness to your creativity and creative life. After all, your creative work, time, and space are sacred.

Having a hard time transitioning into a creative mindset? Use a ritual.

Rituals are effective for marking your transition into your creative space and work, thus making it easier to mentally leave the demands of work and family for a time, especially if you don't have a space dedicated to your creative work. A ritual provides the confidence and focus to break through blocks and make you feel creatively empowered. A ritual, especially used with dreams and journals, is a magical way to connect with your Muse for inspiration, encouragement, and guidance. And, of course, ritual helps you make the transition from your creative space back into daily life.

Whatever ritual you design, know that even the simplest of rituals enhance awareness and can lead to a place of interior quiet, where the voice of the Muse, the "Once upon a time," is heard.

CREATING YOUR OWN RITUAL

Before creating your ritual and gathering the materials and tools you'll use for it, it is important to remember that you are creating the ritual for your purposes, not anyone else's. That means that the ritual—and the materials—can be as minimal and simple or as dramatic and complicated as you like. One caveat, however. If you like the more dramatic and complicated ritual, you might also want to create a simplified version of it for those times when you are too frustrated, tired, or limited on time to perform the more complicated version.

The first step to creating any ritual is to define your intent.

That is, what is the purpose of the ritual? Often, your intent as a creative is to use the ritual as a bridge that helps you move from one state of mind or being to another. For instance, that ritual to move you from your daily life into creation mode. Or from feeling blocked into unblocked. From feeling unmotivated to motivated. Whatever the change or transition you want to make, be sure you have it clearly defined for you.

Since one of the purposes of a ritual is to create a change in consciousness or awareness, think about where you perform the ritual. Sacred or ritual space doesn't necessarily mean having an altar, but you can create one that, again, is as simple or involved as you choose to make it. A simple altar might be no more than a small cloth on which you've placed a candle and a special object such as the photo of a creative role model or mentor, or the strands of yarn you are using in your weaving or other needlework, or a coin that connotes success or financial reward, or a crystal for clarity of vision.

When I am traveling to teach at or attend conferences, I often take a small carved owl (my animal totem), an electric candle (because you can't use a real one in your hotel room), and a small quartz crystal. I create my tiny altar in the room while I am there, then put it away when I am not. Simple in form and content but still effective for helping me ground and center while I breathe and focus on my intent for the day or my gratitude in the evening.

You don't need an altar to make wherever you are working and creating sacred space. One way to do this is to simply imagine drawing a line around you and your work and seeing it illuminate you and your work. Or you can create sacred space with several deep breaths and by focusing on your intention for the time you are working. Or use a drop or two of an essential oil, such as frankincense or lavender or tangerine, in your palms, rub them together, and breathe in the scent, or use it in a diffuser. Another simple ritual is to stand at the threshold of your creative space, then mindfully step over it. You'll learn more about thresholds in another chapter. Sitting down in a particular chair might mark your ritual space. Setting out your laptop and cup of your preferred beverage at a coffee shop defines your ritual and creative space if done mindfully.

Gather any materials you need for your rituals. Unless you have an altar whose elements remain in place, consider using a container to store any ritual materials, such as candles, essential oils, pictures, and more. Then, when you want to do a ritual, you'll be able to easily access the materials or elements you'll need. I carry the elements I mentioned for my traveling altar in a small gift box lined with jeweler's cotton.

A ritual, like a fairy tale, has a clear beginning, middle, and end, often called an opening, a working, and a closing. The opening pulls you into the tale by setting the mood, the middle or working is the heart of the tale, where the action takes place and the magic happens, and the ending or closing is the return home, the happily ever after.

Remember, the tale or the ritual can be as simple or as complex as you want. It can also be as short or as long as you want. The same is true of each part of the ritual, and the ritual may be so short and simple as to seem that there is no beginning, middle, and end.

When designing your rituals, it's important to keep in mind limitations of time and space, and your own energy flow. If you barely have the energy and motivation to do your creative work, you probably are less likely to do a long ritual with many moving parts than if you simply take a couple of deep breaths and light a candle. The ritual is to serve you, not the other way around. Longer, more-complex rituals are great for celebrations of completion and success when you want to hold on to the feelings and perhaps share those moments with others, or for moving through those moments of frustration or dry spells that feel harder to shift. Simple, short rituals are useful for entering or leaving your creative work and space, when you need to center yourself in your work again, or tap into inspiration and guidance in the middle of your work. If this is the first time you are creating and working with rituals, short and simple is better. As you become comfortable with the process, then you can add elements and flourishes that support your intention.

The beginning or opening of a ritual might be one or several deep breaths. It might be lighting a candle, spritzing the air with an essential-oil mist, or turning on a certain piece of music. It might be crossing the threshold into your workspace. Or fixing that hot cup of tea or coffee or hot chocolate.

For the middle or working of the ritual, you might close your eyes and envision what—in the next few moments or hours, days, or months—you want to create, not just with your work but also with your awareness, or with your creative career, or your connection to the Muse. Or you might take the time to look at the picture of a mentor or role model and invoke their creative energy and success. You might carry burning sage or some other incense around your creative workspace, to clear the energies of the space and prepare it for new work. You can also use essential-oil sprays for this.

More practically, the working might include turning off or down your phone. The writing down of concerns, ideas, desires, and doubts on paper or in your journal. It could be getting out your work tools, such as pen and paper, yarns and needles, guitar and picks, or, if you are doing a ritual to transition out of creating, it could be putting away those tools.

The ending or closing can be as simple as the rest. Another deep breath. Picking up a tool. A gesture such as hand to heart. A step across a threshold. Blowing out a candle. Turning off the music. Something that for you and the ritual says, "The End."

Writing friend and celebrant Zita Christian uses this simple ritual that invokes the four elements of earth, air, fire, and water (much like the Magician in the Tarot). When you are having your first cup of coffee or tea or hot chocolate for the day, use your spoon to stir clockwise, drawing in the energy, and think about or say aloud what you want to attract into your day. In that cup and the stirring of the beverage you have the four elements—the air wafting up the steam, the cup made from the earth (as is the spoon), the liquid representing water, and the heat from the element of fire, electrical or gas.

I've included Barbara Biziou's *Joy of Ritual* in the "Resources" section, if you need help shaping a ritual or want to explore ritual further. You can be as imaginative with ritual work as you are with your creative work. Have fun with it, but remember that its purpose is to support you in listening and acting on the Muse's messages, to enacting your own "Once upon a time."

Journal Work

In your journal, make a list of intentions you have for your creative work. List as many as you can think of, such as finishing a chapter, sketching the image on the canvas, composing the next number of measures, facing your fear of failure, finding a new agent. Whatever comes to mind, jot it down.

Next, make a list of anything physical that might represent any or all of those intentions. A sheet of music, a box of charcoals, a gold-paper-covered coin of chocolate (to represent sweet success), the name or image of that ideal agent. The items you list may be universal, like the coin, or uniquely personal.

Finally, write a simple ritual with the form of a beginning, middle, and end. You can use Zita's ritual as an example or write out something like this: Light a candle and take three deep breaths. Speak aloud your intention for the day or for this period of creative work. Place an item or image that invokes that intention next to the candle. Take three more deep breaths. Do your work. Then say, "I give thanks for this time and space and the work I've done today." Blow out or turn off the candle.

You can put the item or image away or leave it next to the candle for the next period of work.

Ritual Work

Use your ritual regularly until you become comfortable with it and don't have to think about it but, rather, can drop into deeper awareness with it. You don't want to be mindless, but mindful. However, you don't want to have to worry about every step in the ritual.

Dreamwork

Though dreamwork will be described and discussed in a future chapter, don't be surprised if your journal and ritual work trigger more dreaming. If that happens, pay attention to them. At the minimum, write down the date and a quick title for it. If you are willing to give time to it, record the dream in present tense.

PART TWO

SLEEPING BEAUTY

THE WISH TO CREATE

A King and Queen longed for a child. Every day they spoke their wish aloud, in their bed chamber, on their royal thrones, in the hall at dinner, even in the gardens as they admired the roses. But no child appeared. Until one day, when the Queen was bathing, a frog climbed out of the water. When she recovered from her surprise, the frog told her she would have a child.

In many fairy tales, a wish triggers the action of the rest of the tale. So much so that the popular Broadway musical and movie *Into the Woods* begins with Cinderella at the grave of her mother. She bemoans the fact that though she's been good and kind, life has not been so to her. She says, "I wish . . ." The spirit of her dead mother sings back to her, "Do you know what you wish? Are you certain what you wish is what you want?"

And, oh, isn't that almost always the challenge? To define what it is you truly want and wish for? For your creative project? For your creative direction or career?

An exhibit, you say? A bestseller? A performance before hundreds if not thousands?

Be careful what you wish for . . .

Years ago, when I started my professional weaving business, I wished to get accepted to the two major wholesale crafts shows in the country. Acceptance involved sending in a certain number of slides for a jury to see and score. I was accepted to one the first time I applied, and eventually, four years later, the other. From that first wholesale show with a thousand exhibitors, my weaving business slowly grew.

My wish was granted, right? Only I didn't really consider what would follow from that wish. That first year, I probably had a dozen wholesale orders from galleries and shops across the country. Those orders added up to hundreds of scarves. Success! Or so I thought.

Except that the chenille scarves that I wove had fringe that was hand-plied and hand-tied. By me. Just tying the fringe took from an hour to five hours or more, depending on the width of the scarf or shawl. Later, as I developed a poncho-like jacket that was 45 inches wide, and throws that were 50 inches wide, tying fringe was something that could take a day of my time. Not to mention the wear and tear on fingers, wrists, and elbows. Because I had priced my work to be competitive with other weavers' work, who weren't doing that type of fringe, I underpriced it to the point where I was barely making $5 an hour.

So be careful what you wish for. That's one of the challenges when it comes to making wishes for our career and our creative projects. What we wish for at the beginning may not be what we wish for at the middle or the end.

Just like the Queen wishing for a child. Would she have wished so persistently for a child if she knew what lay ahead for that child? Probably.

As a mother of three grown sons, I know that when you wish for or dream of having a child, you do so imagining only the sweet and wonderful things about having that child. Even in the discomfort and, for some, extreme challenges of being pregnant, the thought that carries many mothers through is "It will be all worth it when the baby is born."

Ah, but then comes the real work. Sleepless nights (regardless of the child's age), worries about safety and health, and will the child get into the chosen preschool, school, college, and so on. Will they find the right partner? Will they want a partner?

But the Queen doesn't think about this in wishing for a child. She is thinking about giving the King an heir, about wanting a child to love. Note that she doesn't even ask for a boy or a girl. Just a child. And she keeps wishing. Month after month, perhaps year after year.

Then that frog climbs out of the water to tell her that her wish is granted. But why a frog?

The frog has a voice. If you've ever listened to bullfrogs serenade, the song is loud. Other, smaller frogs, such as tree frogs and peepers, are also easily heard, especially when they sing together.

And though you may think, like the princess in the Princess and the Frog, that the frog is such an odd creature to be talking to anyone, let alone deliver a message more in the domain of angels and doctors, it is the frog who tells the Queen she will get her wish. The Queen doesn't ask him how he knows, if he is sure, or how that is possible. She just listens, accepts, and shares the news with the King.

Since they are amphibious, at home both in water and on land, frogs are associated with the magic of water and earth elements, linking them to fairies and elves. They are considered *heralds of abundance and fertility*, perhaps because of the way so many of them appear after a good rain, or because of the many eggs the female frog releases, or because they are most vocal in the spring and early summer. A frog, then, is the perfect messenger for this Queen.

The frog here also symbolizes the movement from emotions and desire (water) to birth and manifestation (earth). This is what happens in the process of creativity. What your heart desires propels you into manifesting it in some form.

Of course, the mind and spirit play a role, but it is the heart that compels. When the heart is not engaged, when you "lose heart," the vitality, the fertility, the abundance of inspiration, and the motivation to create dry up.

Once the frog announces the Queen will give birth, at that point no magic is involved, other than the magic of pregnancy and birth.

The Queen is the one who plays the key role. While the frog is the herald bringing the message of promised birth, it is the Queen (with the King) who wishes and wishes for a child and who then carries that wish, once granted, to fruition. And she does it through two virtues or qualities—persistence and patience.

We can imagine that when they first desired a child, the King and Queen wanted the child immediately (well, within nine months). They didn't expect to have to wait and wait and wait. In that time, they could have given up that wish, and, since this is a fairy tale, the Queen could have sought out a witch or fairy godmother or some other magical being to cast a spell so she could get pregnant and have a child. She could have turned into an animal and disappeared into the forest. Instead, she kept wishing and hoping. She persisted.

Persistence is an often-unrecognized quality of a creative. It can often be the difference between success and failure, between fame and lack of it. You probably know someone in your field who is successful because they persisted in attempting to sell their work, while someone equally or even more talented is not because they didn't keep trying or wishing. They gave up.

The Queen didn't give up. I hope, if you are reading this book, you won't either.

The other quality or virtue that the Queen practiced is patience.

As many times as people talk about overnight success, when you look more closely at that story, you discover stretches of time when the individual worked hard and without recognition to get where they are. You just didn't see the hidden manuscripts, the painted-over landscapes, the filed-away recordings, the failed auditions, or the months spent singing in local dives.

Creativity takes time, in the sharpening of skills, in the development of style, and in the discovery of and connection to an appreciative audience. Lots and lots of time.

Even in that patience and persistence, though, you can imagine that the Queen became discouraged at times. Perhaps that is how she ended up bathing outside in a pond or small lake. She needed to be alone for a while. To be sad. To dream of what she wished for with all her heart. To find a way to wish again and believe that her wish might be granted.

And so the frog appeared to give her a message. The frog was an oracle.

What is an oracle? An oracle is defined as an object through which the divine or a deity makes known its will, whether that is through the symbolic and metaphoric structure of the oracle, such as the Tarot, or the direct inspiration received from such things as flowers or birds (auguries) or stones . . . or frogs.

In modern culture, oracles as messengers from the divine have long been relegated to the fortune-teller's tent. But for creatives, oracles inspire and guide the work. The key to using them is twofold.

First, it is necessary to be as the Queen—willing to attentively listen or see. She didn't discount the message or the messenger because it happened to be a frog. Receiving a message through an oracle, whether a dream, a Tarot card, or the croak of a frog, means being totally present in the moment, able to open the heart to images, ideas, and even voices that seem to arise out of nowhere. To inspiration that comes in unexpected form.

Second, if an oracle "speaks" to you, then be willing to act on it, to enter into a playful yet respectful relationship with it and see where it takes you. When I do a dream consultation, at the end of processing the dream, I ask, "What do you want to do to honor the dream . . . today?" This is to move the dreamer from head-in-the-clouds thinking and daydreaming to directed action that produces immediate change. Now. Today. Not ten weeks or months from now. If you've asked for help or advice from an oracle and received it, then use it!

If you don't know how to work with oracles, don't worry. This isn't about getting it right. It's about getting inspired. It's about connecting your sacred, creative self, through the oracle, with the Muse. Experiment. Explore different oracles. This book shows you how to use dreams as oracles for your creativity, but you can also use the Tarot or other oracle cards, runes, sacred books, birds, or flowers in your garden, or check out the first bumper sticker or shape in the sidewalk or clouds that you see. Whatever causes you to stop, see, and listen, and then patiently work to understand and act on the message.

Look around you. I bet an oracle—perhaps a frog—waits to offer you an inspired message now.

Journal Work

What is it that you truly wish for in your creative project or career? Are you clear about the results if your wish is granted? What will your life or work look like when it comes true? How do you need to prepare for that?

Whether or not you've used oracles before (Tarot or other decks, runes, etc.), what do you want to use now as an oracle for the messenger between you and your Muse? Do you have any concerns about using an oracle? What are they? What signs from the Muse, such as animals or birds appearing in your path, do you want to be alert to? If you haven't been doing this before, you can write in your journal: "Dear Muse, please show me how you'd like to communicate with me." Then pay attention to what shows up. Again, your dreams could become more active. Animals might show up where they normally don't (I had a blue heron standing in my driveway one morning). You might overhear a phrase or word that literally speaks to you. Or a bumper stick or license plate holder might grab your attention. The first time I had an agent with the last name of Goldstein considering my work, I kept seeing cars with license plate holders with the name of a local car dealer . . . Goldstein. She did become my agent.

Write down whatever you see or experience. Don't forget to date it. You might begin to recognize not only repeated oracles, but patterns to them.

Ritual Work

Once you've explored and chosen one or several oracles you want to use, create a ritual for communicating with that oracle. As with other rituals, open with lighting a candle or taking several deep breaths. Quiet the inner chatter, then write in your journal your question for the work or the day, such as "What are the best colors to use in this new painting (or weaving, or design)?" The answer could be the scarlet tanager that flies past your window, or a particularly colorful ad in the magazine you finally decided to flip through before throwing it away.

If you own a Tarot deck, you can try my approach I use when I am working on my novel. Before writing the next scene, I ask a question about it, perhaps where the hero should meet the heroine, while I shuffle the deck of Tarot cards. I pull a few cards, usually three, and then use the images or the implied meanings of the cards to propel me into the scene with a starting image, a new character, or a point of conflict. The cards' purpose is to give me a way to begin, not a structure to limit me. My experience, however, is that they often provide new insights that deepen my story.

Once you have received your answer, record it and ask what you need to do to honor the message. Even if you believe you haven't had an answer yet, give thanks to the Muse, or the Divine for their presence in your work, and then close your ritual.

Dream Work

Pay attention to odd dreams that you may have, especially as relates to animals or people that don't show up in your waking life. They could be there to bring you a message or idea for your work. Don't discount them. Record them simply for now in your dream journal or elsewhere. Date, title, and record the dream in present tense.

THE POWER OF THE TWELFTH FAIRY

What the frog predicted came true, and the Queen was delivered of a beautiful baby girl. The King, understandably, could not contain his joy and ordered a great feast, a celebration. He invited everyone. Or almost everyone. He invited the Wise Women so that they might be kind and think well of the child, perhaps even bless her. Sadly, though there were thirteen Wise Women, the king had only twelve golden plates for them to eat from, so he decided to not invite one of them.

On the day of the feast, people came from far and near to celebrate with the royal family. After everyone had stuffed themselves with all the delicious food and were almost asleep in their seats, the Wise Women rose to give their gifts to the infant princess. One after the other, they magically bestowed upon her every gift a girl could ask for—beauty, grace, charm, riches, and so on.

Then, when eleven of them had given their gifts and the twelfth was ready to take her turn, in swooped the thirteenth. And she wasn't happy. In fact, she was furious, and to avenge herself of the grievous insult, she declared with a loud voice, "On her fifteenth birthday, the King's daughter will prick herself on a spindle and fall down dead." And she swooped out again.

While everyone sat frozen in shock, the twelfth Wise Woman stepped up to the cradle. "While I cannot undo the curse completely, I can and do mitigate it. Your daughter will not die but will fall into a deep sleep that will last for a hundred years.

If you hosted a dinner party for close friends and you wanted to use your good china, how many place settings would you find in your cabinet or cupboard? If you have good china or dinnerware for those special occasions such as birthdays and holidays, then you probably have place settings for twelve. Just like the King and Queen's gold plates.

You certainly don't have place settings for thirteen or nine or any other odd number (unless you've broken some). But what if you end up, somehow, with one more guest to invite than you have settings?

I'd probably use a setting from my everyday dishes for myself, but the King and Queen had a feast with many plates, and they probably wanted to use the twelve gold plates to serve their special guests who would give very special gifts. The King makes that etiquette faux pas because he probably didn't consult with the Queen. She would know better.

In the collection of Grimm fairy tales, certain numbers show up again and again, in the titles and in the stories. Three, four, six, and seven are common, for example: *Goldilocks and the Three Bears*, *The Four Skillful Brothers*, *The Six* (sometimes Seven) *Swans*, *The Wolf and the Seven Little Kids*. The number twelve is used in titles and stories at least five times. A popular example of its use in a title is *The Twelve Dancing Princesses*.

Tracing the significance of the number twelve takes you back to the twelve Greek gods of Olympus, the twelve tribes of Israel, and the twelve apostles of the New Testament of the Bible. Think about how we have twelve months in a year and that our clocks and watches track twelve hours on them. In mystical or numerological terms, twelve is a number of completion, perfection, organization of the whole, and cosmic order.

Over time, the number thirteen has had different connotations, but a common one is bad luck. Perhaps because another association with the number is testing, suffering, or death. The number often symbolizes a transition or dramatic movement from one level to the next. It was also considered unlucky to have thirteen guests at a table, that state of triskaidekaphobia, the fear or avoidance of the number thirteen.

This superstition may have begun with another tale, a Norse myth where the gods were having a party in the halls of Valhalla. As with the fairy tale, someone had not been invited. The god Loki, the trickster god. In his anger, he had a mistletoe-tipped arrow shot at the god Baldr, who was the god of joy, light, and the summer sun. The god died and the whole Earth turned dark.

Loki and the thirteenth Wise Woman break the balance and the cosmic order of twelve. The Wise Woman breaks it by her mere existence, then by her presence at the party, and, finally, with intervening before the Twelfth Wise Woman could give her gift, to give a christening gift of death to Briar Rose.

The thirteenth Wise Woman throws a spanner into the works. Everything was going along smoothly and then . . . bang! The wicked fairy shows up and doesn't even wait her turn to give her gift. She pushes ahead of the twelfth Wise Woman, breaking the order to curse the infant to death. A celebration of new life is suddenly the cause for death. She casts the spell and thereby throws the life and story of Briar Rose off onto a new path.

Breaking the order. One of the roles of the creative. To break the balance and the cosmic order, to upset the apple cart and throw things off into a new direction. If balance and the cosmic order, the status quo, were maintained, nothing new would be created or invented. That would, in fact, be the curse of death.

Note that the twelfth Wise Woman doesn't wail and gnash her teeth because of the curse the other one placed. She doesn't shrug her shoulders and say that she can't do anything, that it's all beyond her control. No, instead she admits what she can't do—eliminate the curse entirely—but takes control and does what she can do—mitigate the curse.

As with the Sleeping Beauty, someone in your young life may have cast a spell on you that meant your creative dreams and desires were destroyed, distorted, or hidden away. All that beauty and joy and excitement cursed to death.

When I was in elementary school, the music teacher told me I had a wonderful voice. Later, in high school, some teenage boys made fun of my singing (and isn't that the way of teenagers of either gender). Even as they hurt my feelings, what kept me singing was the comment that music teacher made to me years previously.

While in college studying creative writing, I had a teacher who mocked and tore apart a short story I wrote about a young woman missing her husband and seeking connection and solace from nature. Now, it would be called speculative fiction. Then, the prof called it sentimental drivel. Fortunately, I had two other writing professors who complimented me on my writing. One of them went so far as to tell me in a personal conversation that of all the students in the class, he felt I understood story and would be the person to continue writing and eventually publish.

While being able to sing may not be critical in my creative life now, the writing is, and how fortunate I am to have had two other Wise Men mitigate the spell cast on me by the other one. These are personal examples of how easy it is for someone to cast the spell of creative death.

In storytelling terms, the thirteenth Wise Woman's spell is the inciting incident that sets the rest of the tale in motion. In astrological terms, the spell might be seen as the influence of the planet Uranus, triggering something unexpected. In the Tarot, it's the Tower card, shaking the foundations of accepted structures and ideas. The "inciting incident," the spell, can be anything that sets you onto your creative desires or tosses you away from them.

What is a spell? A spell is a combination or group of specific words with a solid intent and concentrated focus to direct energy toward a certain outcome. In magic, the way to concentrate the focus is to use a wand, like Harry Potter or Hermione Granger. Creatives use their fingers, their pens, their brushes, their toes, their chisels, and more. You might not use words to cast the spell. You might use notes or gestures or colors or sounds, which have a solid intent toward a certain outcome.

As a creative, you cast spells on a regular basis since you are the Magician. Remember?

And, just like Mickey Mouse in "The Sorcerer's Apprentice" segment of *Fantasia* or Ron's backfiring "Eat Slugs!" spell in *Harry Potter and the Chamber of Secrets*, not all creative spells work quite in the way they are meant to. When working magic, sometimes the spell doesn't work because . . . well, because the intent isn't clear, the focus isn't concentrated, or the outcome is too defined or not defined enough.

And sometimes, even though the outcome may be sufficiently defined, just as with magic and spells, the outcome isn't always what is imagined or expected, regardless of preparation, intent, and actions.

Because of this, Briar Rose becomes a tale worth telling, an experience worth sharing. Without the curse, the princess would have lived a glamorous, unchallenged life. Her happily ever after would have been diminished by the lack of any challenge or conflict, of any tears and sorrow. Together, the thirteenth and twelfth Wise Women change her life in an unexpected way. And not just her life, but everyone's in the castle.

It's also important to remember that as evil as she seems in the story, the thirteenth fairy or Wise Woman had a necessary role to play as catalyst and test. But more about her later when she greets Briar Rose on her sixteenth birthday.

Journal Work

Twelfth fairies can make a huge difference. Do you know who your twelfth fairies are? Have you let them and their encouragement be forgotten while you focus on all the thirteenth fairies who have cursed you and your work? Make a list of your thirteenth wise women (or men) and the twelfth wise women (or men) who helped mitigate their curses.

Ritual Work

Light a candle or breathe in an uplifting or strengthening essential oil such as grapefruit or peppermint. Write down the negative messages you've received about your creative work, the curses cast upon you. Use paper and pen. Consider playing some soothing or uplifting music while you do this. Then, remembering some of your twelfth fairies, right down on another sheet of paper a few of the mitigating spells, the compliments you've received on your work and your imagination.

Now, preferably outside, burn the sheet with the curses, then bury or spread the ashes knowing that Earth will transform (as in a fairy tale) those ashes to something nurturing and useful. Or, if you've written the curses on dissolving paper, put them in a bowl of water, then pour the water onto the earth.

Then, read aloud the mitigating spells, those words that speak to the beauty, power, and magic that is your creativity. Read them slowly so you take in the words. You can keep the sheet somewhere near your workspace or on your altar to remind you.

Finally, give thanks for those twelfth fairies and end the ritual, turning off or blowing out the candle and taking a few deep breaths.

Dreamwork

Continue to record any sleep dreams (or nightmares) that you remember. Look for the twelfth fairy, anyone who is a helper in the dream. Not asking for help is a challenge for many, especially women, because they've been raised to give help, not ask for or receive it. Pay attention to whether or not you think to ask for help in your dreams.

ENTERING THE TOWER

The King, like any loving parent, was determined to protect his precious child and therefore commanded that every spindle and spinning wheel in the kingdom be burnt. And so the child grew, manifesting all the gifts of beauty and grace and wisdom that had been bestowed upon her by the Wise Women.

Nevertheless, as much as parents prefer to think that they can protect their children from harm—from life—the day came when Briar Rose was to celebrate her fifteenth birthday. Some say her parents left her alone in the castle that day; some say they were distracted with the preparations for her birthday party. But whatever the reason, Briar Rose found herself free to explore the castle, letting her curiosity lead her where it may, which was to an old tower she had never noticed before. Dank and dusty though it was, she was too curious, and so she climbed the winding stairs until she reached the top and found a door with a rusty key and lock.

With youthful determination and strength, she forced the key to turn and the door to open. And drawn by the hum of a large wheel, she crossed the threshold and stepped into the room.

The urge to protect is common to parents, whether four-legged or two-legged. That urge is necessary in order to ensure the survival of the species.

Early-childhood curses on your creativity might compel you to be overprotective of your creative dreams. After all, it is so much easier and safer to just keep those dreams in your imagination, where there is no such thing as failure or criticism or rejection. You don't have to worry whether you have the wherewithal, the commitment, or the endurance to actually create what you imagine. In your mind, in your imagination, everything comes up roses.

Most creative dreams start in childhood, where there are yet no limitations, no questions of how, but only the desire to explore and discover and create.

I remember carefully molding clay (there was no Play-Doh) into a model of the Garden of Eden. Where my abilities failed my vision, my mother occasionally gave me a hand. I remember making a doll's hat out of cardboard and strips of fabric with my great-grandmother. And I remember being seven and making my very first book out of paper and staples or tape, with my story and illustrations.

Those creations were about childhood enthusiasm and curiosity and discovery.

The very things that parents often try to direct, redirect, and control, sometimes out of their own personal stories and fears, sometimes out of a desire to keep you safe, to help you avoid "the pricking."

And yet, if you've been a parent—or a son or daughter—then you know that the only thing that helps a child grow strong and able to survive are all the hurts and disappointments, the bumps and bruises—and even scars—one inevitably acquires in the course of growing up.

Even princesses can't spend their entire lives in a bubble. And, typically, the minute that parental surveillance slips, the princess goes on an adventure.

Creativity, especially in its early stages, even under the tutelage of a mentor, is an exploration that means both successes and failures, bumps and bruises, and messes that need to be cleaned up.

Creativity, at every stage, requires curiosity and that question "I wonder if . . ."

Walt Disney said, "We keep moving forward, *opening new doors* (italics mine), and doing new things, because we're curious, and curiosity keeps leading us down new paths."

Eleanor Roosevelt said, "I think, at a child's birth, if a mother could ask a fairy godmother to endow it with the most useful gift, that gift should be curiosity."

At whatever age a person begins to explore their creativity, curiosity is a necessary element, pushing one to try this, reject that, consider another.

Certainly, curiosity led Sleeping Beauty into a place she'd never been before and into circumstances she probably couldn't have prepared for. You do wonder, though, don't you? Had no one warned her of the curse? Or, like most teenagers, had she decided that everyone else was being silly, that they were old fogies, and she would just investigate for herself?

If she had been warned, then she was not just curious—she was rebellious and a rule breaker, characteristics necessary for deep creative exploration. Picasso followed the groundbreaking work of Paul Cézanne by ignoring the rules of perspective, proportion, and depth. Women artists and writers broke the rules that insisted only men had the artistic eye or voice. Think of what we would have missed out on without female rule breakers such as artists Mary Cassatt, Georgia O'Keeffe, and Frida Kahlo; authors such as Mary Shelley, Jane Austen, Harriet Beecher Stowe, and Octavia Butler; composers such as St. Hildegard of Bingen, Zitkála-Šá (Lakota: Red Bird), and Carole King; and many more dancers, actors, and others.

Breaking rules isn't easy, but curiosity and the rebellious nature of a teenager helps. If you find yourself stuck in time or a rut, look at where you might be following rules too closely as a way to break free. "I wonder . . ." and "What if . . ." are effective ways to trigger curiosity and open doors to creativity.

So, we last left Briar Rose climbing the stairs of the tower. That tower. In some studies or examinations of the story, the tower is considered a phallic symbol, because once she arrives at the top of the tower, she is about to lose her innocence as a child with the pricking of her finger.

But, in shamanic terms, especially for dreamwork, that climb up the tower is understood as moving from the natural plane or world to the upper world. The upper world is the place of the superconscious or superego. And in terms of other spiritual traditions, it is a climb to the spiritual level or realm. In the Tarot, the Tower is an archetypal symbol for the breaking up of old structures in order to undergo transformation. That climb up those stairs is significant for our heroine—and you. It is a means of reaching out to a source of divine inspiration, of connection with the Muse.

Often, in early stages of a creative project, that's the first goal, to connect with the Muse, to inspiration. Elizabeth Gilbert, author of *Eat, Pray, Love*, shares in her 2013 TED Talk that in ancient Greece and Rome, people did not believe that creativity came from inside a person, but that creativity was "this divine attendant spirit that came to human beings from some distant and unknowable source for some distant and unknowable reasons." According to Gilbert, the Greeks called the spirit a daemon (not a demon) and the Romans called it a genius. Gilbert saw her responsibility to her creativity was to show up and be responsive. It was the daemon's or genius's job to inspire.

To connect to the Muse—or the daemon or genius—first you, like Briar Rose, must show up and cross the threshold.

A threshold is that line, actual or implied, between one place and another, one state and another, one phase or age and another. The most commonly understood example of a threshold is the one that the groom carries the bride over into their new home. One side of the threshold is their lives as singles, independent of one another. The other side of the threshold is their life as a committed couple.

In storytelling, the threshold often marks the place between acts (as in a stage play). Usually, the first act shows the hero or heroine in their life as it is in that moment. The threshold or break from act 1 to act 2 marks the movement of the character and the story from the old life to the new life or adventure. Think of Frodo leaving his hobbit hole to go adventuring. Or Harry Potter getting on the train at the station. The train is one long threshold crossing, a liminal time and space where he is neither at his home nor at Hogwarts. Think of Dorothy waking up after the tornado and walking out of her house into Oz.

Frequently, in addition to the threshold, there is a threshold guardian, someone or something that tests the character's resolve to cross the threshold and move forward. For Harry, one of the guardians was the station number. Was he willing to push forward through what appeared to be a solid brick wall, as he saw other Hogwarts students do? For Dorothy, the guardian was Glenda the Good Witch of the North. She was there to make sure that Dorothy's intentions were good and that she wouldn't harm the Munchkins.

For Briar Rose, there is no apparent guardian except that rusty lock. Is her curiosity strong enough to move her forward?

For you, the climb inward and upward for inspiration brings you to the threshold between your "normal" life and the life as creative. Guardians show up in different forms. Sometimes, what tests you are family members or pets demanding time and attention. Or the chores piled up and staring you in the face. Or the ringing phone. Or the job.

Each time you are ready to do your work, these guardians test to see if your intent is serious or just a flight of fancy, a whim of curiosity. And, as you may have experienced, the tests occur at critical moments for you, when life is already demanding more than enough of your time and energy, when you think you don't have one iota of anything left to give to anyone. You may have to fight your way past those threshold guardians. But you can also use your creativity here. Is there a way to dance or play with them? Or to compromise? An hour of your work in exchange for a walk, or a phone call, or fifteen minutes of paperwork.

The tests will always, with rare exceptions, be there. Are you curious enough? Is the desire to create undeniable?

Here, the Wise Woman raises her gaze from her spinning and waits to see . . . will you cross that threshold or not?

Journal Work

What do you remember creating as a child, with curiosity, enthusiasm, and play?

What thresholds have you crossed in your life? Who or what were the guardians? How did you deal with them?

What thresholds have you crossed with your creativity? Who or what were the guardians? How did you deal with them? When did you fail to cross a threshold because of the intimidation of the guardian(s)?

Ritual Work

Design a small, brief ritual that you can use for crossing a threshold, particularly when you want to do your creative work, and that you can do anytime, anywhere. A ritual that doesn't require candles or anything else but you. For example, you might whistle a tune, or draw an imaginary line with your finger and then step over it.

Dreamwork

A key to working with dreams is a sense of wonder and curiosity. When I teach or work with clients, the quickest, most common question is "What is the dream about?" That's often just a mild curiosity. Instead of that generalized question, look back over a couple of your dreams and be specifically curious. Consider the questions "I wonder . . ." or "What if . . ." For example, "I wonder why the fox is black instead of red?" Play with those questions and elements of your dreams. Be alert to ideas and insights that lead to inspiration.

THE SPINNING WHEEL OF TIME

In the room stood an old woman, bent of back, with gnarled fingers. Slowly, she stepped back and forth in a rocking motion, turning a large wheel with one hand while drawing strands of fiber with the other onto another part of the mechanism, which was set in motion by the spinning of the large wheel. "Oh," Briar Rose said, approaching the wheel and the old woman, "whatever are you doing there?"

"I am spinning," answered the old woman. "Would you like to try it?"

"What is this that turns and rattles so merrily?" Briar Rose asked, and she reached out to touch, and her finger, instead of touching the thread, landed on the very sharp spindle, pricking her finger so that a drop of blood welled forth.

"Oh," Briar Rose cried, shocked and surprised, "oh, oh." Suddenly light of head, and weak in the knees, she staggered, and the old woman guided her to a soft bed that was there.

"Here, dearie, you rest here. Sleep. Sleep long and well."

She dropped her disguise and stood in her youthful form of the thirteenth fairy. Chuckling, she pulled the coverlet over the girl. "Sleep long, and perhaps not so well."

Throughout the castle, as if everyone else had also pricked their fingers, all fell asleep where they were, in stable and kitchen and armory and throne room, where the King and Queen sat, having just returned from their travels. All the animals slept too. As did the fires.

Briar Rose stepped over the threshold and approached the spinning wheel, something she has never seen before, because unbeknown to her, her father had all the spinning wheels burned. Curiosity led her around the castle, to the tower and into the room. Now the Fates take over.

Spinning is one of the most ancient of crafts, followed by knitting and netting and weaving. String, rope, and thread are essential not only for clothing but for the many tasks ancient and new of survival and comfort, such as tying up a boat, catching fish, setting a snare, staying warm during sleep, storing goods, and more. Like other textile arts, especially weaving, spinning is, because of its necessity and existence across cultures, prevalent both in myth and fairy tale.

At first, fibers were twisted between fingers, resulting in threads or string no longer than a handspan. Then a spindle, a stick or rod of a certain length with a whorl or circular piece of wood toward one end, came into use. The spindle could be spun and dropped, which sent the twist up through the fibers held in the other hand, or rolled along the leg, with the spinner sitting on the floor or ground. The spinning wheel appeared in the 1300s and took several forms depending on the fiber to be spun. Flax was often spun on a walking wheel like the one described above.

Because spinning occurs in most cultures, so do myths and fairy tales of spinning. Among the Navajo of the Southwest, there is Grandmother Spider, and the spider also shows up prominently in Greek myth in the story of Arachne and Athena. Athena turns the mortal Arachne into a spider for her hubris in her weaving.

In Egyptian myths, Isis teaches spinning, and Neith is the goddess of spinning and weaving, as is the goddess Tayet; in China, Chih-Nii is the goddess of spinning, weaving, and the clouds; in Incan myth, Mama Ocllo teaches women to spin; and in Europe, spinning goddesses appear in Norway, Britain, Germany, and more.

In addition to the story of Athena and Arachne, there are also the three Greek Fates: Clotho, Lachesis, and Atropos. Clotho spins the thread of a mortal's life, Lachesis measures it, and Atropos cuts it. Atropos is the oldest of the three Fates and is known as "the Inflexible One." Once she decided to cut the thread of life, no one could make her change her mind, not even all-powerful Zeus.

This inflexibility is represented in the fairy tale by the Twelfth Wise Woman's inability to totally counteract the Thirteenth Wise Woman's spell. The Twelfth could mitigate it but not sufficiently alter or undo it. Instead of final death, Briar Rose experiences *le petit mort*, "the little death," as sleep is sometimes referred to, because of the loss of consciousness. Only this is no small death. Sleeping Beauty will not wake in a few hours or even a few days but will instead sleep for one hundred years—as in many of the sleeping-hero tales.

Spinning is also used to suggest the spinning of stories or the spinning out of creative projects. Three is considered a number of magic, the Goddess, and creativity and is frequently seen in myth and fairy tale, even more often than the numbers twelve and thirteen. Think of "The Three Little Pigs," "The Three Billy Goats Gruff," or "Goldilocks and the Three Bears." Words and actions in the tales are often repeated three times; one of the reasons for this was that it made it easier to remember the story.

Also, as with stage plays and most forms of modern storytelling, this fairy tale is divided into three stages or acts. The first act is the birth, curse, and growth of Sleeping Beauty. The second act is her falling asleep for a hundred years and the decision of the right prince at the right time to find the sleeping princess and break the spell. The third act, or the denouement, is the prince's kiss, her awakening, the castle's awakening, and the wedding and celebration of Sleeping Beauty's return to life.

At this point in the story, though, Briar Rose is confronted by the Thirteenth Wise Woman. To Briar Rose, this is just an old woman doing something new; again, something she hadn't seen done before. She sees the fibers moving from the distaff, spinning into a thread and onto the bobbin. How is that happening? Because of her wonderful, creative characteristic of curiosity, she reaches out to see what that spinning mechanism is about.

She has reached out to touch her fate. The Thirteenth Wise Woman represents one of the Greek goddesses of time and fate, Atropos, and the wheel represents the Wheel of Time.

Everyone is at the mercy of the Wheel of Time. If you are a professional artist, writer, performer, or other creative, you are constantly riding the Wheel of Time to attend auditions or practices or to meet deadlines. If you are not a professional (and even if you are), you may deal with Time when you have to stop creating to feed the family, or go to the 9–5 job, or serve on a committee.

Time is a big challenge for creatives. I hear this often from women who struggle to make their work and themselves a priority. I hope this is changing among young women, but many women have been raised to believe that putting their needs ahead of others is selfish. Whether it is a child wanting attention, a husband wanting a meal, or a community organization wanting bookkeeping or a batch of cookies, women tend to put those requests or demands first, figuring they'll get to their creativity in a little while. Without boundaries (such as a hedge) or removing oneself from the normal environment (such as to a tower), pretty soon a little while becomes a hundred days and then, in a sense, a hundred years (i.e., never). I've seen this happen over and over. That Wheel of Time helps cast a spell, sometimes to your detriment.

Writers joke about needing to tell family members, "Unless you are bleeding (profusely) or the house is on fire, don't interrupt me."

While that is an example of writer hyperbole, it does get across the message that whatever you are being interrupted for had better be serious. Anything that can wait should wait.

Ironically, while you might have to deal with Time in your daily life, when you are in creative flow, time disappears altogether, as if you've stepped into a dream, and the world around you falls asleep. Until someone comes knocking on the studio door or calls you on the phone. Then you are jarred out of timelessness to ride the Wheel of Time once again.

And so it is that Sleeping Beauty, affected by the Wheel of Time, her fifteenth birthday, meets her Fate and, in the enactment of the spell, slips into a place without time. Although her time as an adolescent is ending, her time as a creative adult is beginning. The Thirteenth Wise Woman serves as psychopomp, from Greek mythology, the one who guides the souls of the dead to the Underworld or guides the souls of the living into the realm of dreams and spirit.

The enchantment has begun. Briar Rose and the world around her falls asleep, asleep to time and its demands, which is why even the cooking fires sleep. No one and nothing needs anything from Briar Rose. Her family won't come looking for her, nor will servants. She won't miss a meal.

Time has stopped. She has entered that space of dreams and timelessness. A place of creative freedom and limitless possibilities.

Journal Work

What are the demands on your time? What have you committed to? What demands are made because you haven't established boundaries or defined expectations?

Have you set boundaries so that when you are in your creative space, you aren't interrupted? While you may not use the bleeding and fire example, you might set a timer for family members and silence your phone. What do you need to do to honor your time with your creativity?

How many hours a week do you allow yourself for your creativity? Is it enough?

Ritual Work

Once a week, mark off time on your calendar for your creativity. If something comes up during the week, try to reschedule your creative time just as you would a doctor's appointment. As you set aside the time, think about how your creativity is important and that your time with it is sacred. Write out a mantra or affirmation that confirms your right to create. Repeat it when you do the scheduling. Repeat it when others try to steal your creative time. Make a bumper sticker of it and hang it where you—and maybe the family—can see it.

Remember that as you model how to honor your creative time, you do the same for those around you. This is especially important if you have children. Though they may complain at first or be too young to understand, they will learn to do the same for themselves. And that is a wonderful thing.

Dreamwork

Your task here is to make sure that for at least a couple of weeks you keep to a schedule for bedtime and rising time. Not only do you generally sleep better when you keep to a routine (i.e., work with Time instead of against it), but better sleep usually means more-active dreaming. Just as you schedule time for your creativity, see if you can schedule regular time for sleep. If you are the parent of a new baby or sick child, well, set this as a goal to work toward once the child is older or healthy. If you change shifts at work, try to maintain a regular sleep schedule for the time you do sleep.

SACRED SPACE FOR SLEEPING
AND DREAMING

While the people and animals and fires and even the trees around the castle fell into a deep slumber, a great hedge sprang up that circled the castle and its environs completely. The thorns of the hedge were long and sharp, and each year the hedge grew higher and higher, so nothing of the castle could be seen, not even the flag flying from the highest point of the highest tower, the tower where the beauteous Briar Rose slept.

It wasn't until I was an adult and part of a dream circle working both with conscious and sleep dreams that I saw Briar Rose's sleep as more than a long night's sleep.

After teaching the techniques for working with both types of dreaming to a group of writers at a weeklong conference for several summers, I decided to use the fairy tale as the metaphor for writers' dreaming, understanding that Beauty's sleep was so much more than is usually acknowledged. For me, it didn't make sense that she just lay there inert, waiting for some unknown prince. Of course, she wasn't really even waiting because she was in that timeless space of sleep and dreams.

But if you had nothing else to do but lie in bed, wouldn't you dream? Even if you were awake, wouldn't you lie there and daydream? Maybe about the next book or painting or other project? Maybe about what it would be like to take your creative career to the next level? You'd do more than count the cracks in the old castle ceiling, wouldn't you?

Your bed has the potential to be as much a place of magic and creative production as your studio or work area. But in order for you to maximize the gifts of sleeping and dreaming, you have to design your bed and bedroom to do more than let you catch twenty z's.

The average person spends a third of their life sleeping. But you aren't just sleeping, you are also dreaming. Some experts believe that lack of sufficient REM (rapid-eye-movement) sleep and the dreaming that occurs with it may actually be the cause of many health problems for Americans. Dreaming is that important. But it's also important as a source of inspiration and guidance for your creative work.

To ensure a good night's sleep and to sleep as if cursed (or blessed?) to do it for a hundred years, the following suggestions will help you create a cozy nest.

ELIMINATE ANYTHING FROM THE BEDROOM THAT MIGHT DISTURB YOUR SLEEP.

If you can, move your TV and computer out of the bedroom or house them in a cabinet you can close at night. Televisions and computers are two things that can throw off your sleep routine by getting you involved in a show, video game, or work so that you go to sleep later than usual. Late-night news or doing work on your computer could create stress— not a good state in which to try to fall asleep. If you can't or don't want to move them out of your bedroom, and you don't have a cupboard in which to enclose them, then consider covering them with a pretty scarf or some other fabric. Let them sleep while you sleep.

Be aware of light in the bedroom. Get rid of or cover anything that emits light while you sleep. Our bodies have a natural twenty-four-hour cycle of biochemical, physiological, and behavioral processes called the circadian rhythm. Light plays an enormous role in that rhythm, so the quality of our sleep—and our health—can be affected by the light present in our rooms at night, especially if you are one of those people who sleeps with a digital clock staring you in the face, and more so if that light is white or blue. Replace the digital clock with an old-fashioned alarm clock, or put the clock on a shelf below the level of the mattress so it isn't shining in your face. When I travel, I'll cover the hotel clock with a hand towel. Be creative with this. You'll sleep better and feel more rested.

Imagine that you are Sleeping Beauty. What does your bedroom look like? Surely, it's not dirty or cluttered?

And if it is, do what you can to clean up, organize, and get rid of clutter. Clutter, trash, piles of dirty laundry, and stacks of papers and books are stagnant energy. Every time you look at them, some part of your mind is making a list of all the things you should be doing about them instead of resting or imagining your next creation. Clutter is NOT conducive either to good sleep (or sexy lovemaking). If you find you like to have a lot of books close at hand for reading before bed, then get a small bookcase or book shelf and keep your books and dream and other journals there. Minimize clutter on dressers and tabletops. Use small trays for perfume bottles and makeup. Antique cups or handcrafted bowls make lovely catchalls for jewelry and change. Just be sure not to let them fill up with things that aren't used regularly. Try to keep the bedroom as uncluttered as possible. It is hard to focus on our partner or relax into sleep if our bedrooms are cluttered and we constantly face reminders of things we need to do.

MAKE THE SPACE AS SPECIAL AND LUXURIOUSLY WELCOMING TO YOUR SENSES AS POSSIBLE.

Do the colors on your walls make you feel cheerful or restful? Some colors are too energizing, such as bright reds, oranges, and yellows, although the deep, shaded tones of those colors work for some people. While red may be the color of passion, it needs to be the right color, since red is also the color of anger and blood. The cool colors— green, blue, lavender—are generally more calming, especially in the lighter shades. Be sure the color is something you like, that evokes a sense of luxury and tranquility.

Pay attention to what you hang on the walls. Do you really want to sleep beneath that photograph of a raging fire? Or that rubbing of a graveyard tombstone? Think about the images you are seeing as you prepare for bed and when you wake in the morning. Choose the ones that delight your eyes and your imagination, that take you to serene places or inspire romance. Photos of loved ones also create that safe and loving feeling.

You want your bed, pillows, and bed linens to be as comfortable as you can afford. Pillows wear out about every six months. Mattresses need to be turned regularly and vacuumed to eliminate dust mites. And they need to be replaced on an average of ten years. Buy the kind of sheets that create the texture you like— crisp, silky, soft—because just like the visuals of your room, texture and touch are important as well. Think about warm rugs under bare feet, or cool bare floors. Velvety spreads or throws.

Use oils, mists, and flowers to pleasantly scent your bedroom. Studies have shown that lavender and jasmine are two scents that are particularly supportive of a good night's sleep, with lavender being particularly effective for women. Other helpful oils include chamomile, bergamot, sandalwood, and mandarin. If you don't have allergies, an arrangement of flowers appeals both to the eyes and nose and adds to that feeling of luxury.

Keep the temperature a little on the cool side. We sleep better when the bedroom temperature is between 60 and 68 degrees. Any warmer tends to make for a restless night's sleep (and uncomfortable lovemaking).

Lest this seem unnecessary, remember that not only does a soothing, clean, organized room help you sleep, but it is appealing to the senses, and feeding the senses also feeds your creativity.

CREATE BEDTIME RITUALS THAT HELP SLOW YOU DOWN AND READY YOU FOR SLEEPING AND DREAMING.

Set the stage with lighting. What is the mood you want to create? One of seduction and love? One of rest and renewal? Or are you preparing yourself to enter the dreamtime? It's great if you have lighting that is adaptable to all those purposes.

Regular candles are nice for a romantic mood or for meditation, but be sure to extinguish them before you fall asleep. Battery-operated candles are a safe option, and you can purchase ones that flicker, and some have remote timers. They come in a variety of sizes and colors.

Set the stage for sleep with scent. Mist your bed with one of your chosen scents— lavender or vanilla for relaxing, or sandalwood or rose for dreaming. And, of course, rubbing on a body oil of one of these scents, or a blend, would be wonderful as well. Or rub your chosen oil on the soles of your feet. The skin on the bottoms of our feet is the most permeable, so the oils are absorbed more quickly.

Finally, consider adding the element of music. Whether you are sliding into bed to read, relax, make love, or sleep and dream, music is a great aid. If you find music too distracting for falling asleep, choose a recording of your most soothing sound, such as ocean waves, or water burbling over rocks, or the sound of crickets and owls— whatever helps you relax and drift off.

CREATE TRANSITIONS FOR THE MIND AND BODY TO MOVE FROM ACTIVITY INTO SLEEP.

Take a hot bath or shower. The drop in temperature after you get out of the shower or bath signals your body it is time for bed, because your body temperature drops to its lowest level when you are sleeping.

Wear socks to bed. Or put a microwavable heat pack at your feet. Because our feet are the farthest from our hearts, they tend to be prone to poor circulation, so warming them up before sleep will mean a less restless night of sleep (and a bed partner who will be grateful when you stop using their legs as your heating pad).

Be careful what you read before bed. Try reading something entertaining, or spiritually uplifting. Or try doing crosswords. That approach lets you fall asleep without any images in your mind that might interfere with or influence your dreams or disturb your sleep. These steps will help you have a deep and relaxing REM sleep, the sleep phase that leads to dreaming.

You can use these same elements to design a space for your creativity that supports you rather than distracts you or makes you anxious. An additional element that is important in the area where you create is organization. Only you can determine what is just the right amount of chaos and what is too much. If you need help but can't afford to hire a professional organizer or don't want one in your space, then there are numerous shows on television and videos on YouTube with plenty of organization ideas. One of my favorite books on organizing is *Organizing for the Creative Person* by Dorothy Lehmkuhl and Dolores Cotter Lamping. The authors understand that some clutter is natural to a creative, and they offer organizing principles and solutions with that in mind.

One of the most important elements of a bedroom, at least if you live in a home with other people, is a door, preferably one that locks when you need absolute, uninterrupted privacy.

These steps will help your bedroom and bed feel like they are fit for the royalty that you are, and for the dreams of your royal self. When Briar Rose fell under the spell of slumber, her physical body was vulnerable while she slept and dreamed. The same was true of all those in the castle environs. So a great hedge of thorns sprang up to surround and protect it all. If someone were to wake, they could explore the castle and its grounds but go no further. And, until the time was right, no one could penetrate the hedge to see if the tales and rumors about a Sleeping Beauty were true or not.

The hedge acted as a necessary physical boundary.

You need to establish physical boundaries as well, when you are dreaming and creating.

If you are dreaming—in your bed or doing conscious dreaming elsewhere—you need to protect yourself. You can do that physically by closing a door, putting on headphones to listen to recorded drumming that overrides other sounds, or putting up a sign. You can do it energetically by using burning sage or other incense to mark your circle of dreaming, or you can draw a circle around you with your finger. You can use both physical and energetic actions to set a boundary.

As mentioned in the last chapter, another big challenge for my clients and maybe for you is setting a boundary around your creative workspace, especially if you work at home. Working at home is tricky if you don't have a separate room. Closing a door is a definite sign you don't want to be disturbed, but what to do if you don't have a room with a door?

If you work from home and have children or parents whom you care for, establishing boundaries around your creative space may feel impossible. As a parent, I know how tempting creative materials can be to children, so think about how you can create a visual sign or barrier that tells everyone, "This is my work. Leave it—and me—alone."

Years ago, Martha Stewart showed how to use a cupboard to create a sewing area. She's since done closets and craft furniture. The idea is to use what you have in an imaginative way to organize your materials and establish a space for your creative work. If, however, you work in clay, or iron, or hot glass, or—as I used to do—on large looms, then you will need more space than a corner chair and table, or a renovated cupboard. If you can't put your work away or store it in a basket or bench, get a beautiful blanket or throw and cover your work. Make touching that blanket and the work a definite no-no.

Some arts and crafts necessitate a dedicated workspace. In recent years, the coworking spaces have sprung up around the world. The spaces aren't just for office-type use. Artists and other creatives have adapted the idea for their purposes as well, targeted at musicians, painters, architects, dancers, and more, with amenities geared toward their interests. In my area, one coworking space rented for $20 a day and for $200 for the month.

But whether in the home, in a cupboard, or in a shed, or at a coworking space, establish that space as yours. And let others know not to intrude or enter without an invitation.

Pretend there's a high hedge of thorns around it.

Journal Work

Do you protect your creative space? Have you demarcated a space that is primary for your creative work? If not, why not? What can you do to correct that or to better protect your space? Do you need to add a space by finishing off an area in your home or buying a shed or renting in a coworking space?

Ritual Work

Design a ritual that affirms your right to a creative space that supports you and motivates you.

Dreamwork

This is daydream work. Let yourself imagine your ideal creative space. See the space and elements in it. Imagine your tools and materials neatly organized. A large space for you to work in. A place to sit and sketch or write or think. As you scan the space, what is one element in that space that you could bring into your current area or space of creative work? Something not too big or expensive. Something you might already have somewhere in your home. Bring that element into your space to honor you and the work you do and to make the ideal creative space more real.

ENTERING THE REALM OF DREAMS

Briar Rose wasn't in the castle tower any more with the strange old woman and her spinning wheel, but she didn't know where she was. In a forest with trees whispering above her, and an owl blinking down at her from a branch that stretched over her head. An owl with white feathers and gold eyes that stared at her. It bent its head to preen its feathers, and when its head came back up, a white feather drifted through the air to land at her feet.

When Briar Rose falls asleep, she both sleeps and dreams, carried into the realm of the unconscious by the spell, much as Christine travels by boat into the underground realm of the Phantom in *Phantom of the Opera*.

In sleep, everyone dreams, regardless of whether or not they remember their dreams. Some people, understandably, don't want to remember their dreams because of past traumas such as military service, abuse, or other forms of violence. But if you would like to access and remember your sleep dreams for your creative work or for your personal life (or both), here are some tips to help you do just that.

Avoid alcohol, caffeine, and overeating.
These disturb your sleep patterns, therefore affecting your dreams and your ability to remember them.

If your mind feels in a jumble before bed, then get it out on the page.
Write down what is tossing about in your mind in sentences or in lists, such as

what you have to do the next day. Do a "brain dump" in order to make room for the dreams.

Keep a journal and pen by the bed to record your dreams.
It is too easy to forget your dreams once you move into your day. Having a dream journal within easy reach means you can capture the dream immediately upon awakening, while it is still fresh in your mind. And it tells the dream messengers that you take them seriously.

Set an intention to dream.
Write the next day's date at the top of the next blank page in your journal and write the request for a dream. If you want to incubate a dream, then ask a specific question to think about as you fall asleep, such as "What needs to happen in the next movement of my symphony or the next scene of my book?" Then allow yourself to drift off to sleep thinking about it.

Avoid using a loud alarm, if possible.
You want to be able to move slowly and gently out of sleep and dreaming. If you need an alarm to wake you, consider using soft, nonverbal music, or the sounds of nature, such as water flowing. For years, my husband woke to the alarm to get up for work when a popular PBS radio program opened with the sound of birds singing and chirping away.

Don't move as you come awake.
If you want to be able to remember and record any dreams from the night, one of the keys is to *not move*. Something about the effects of gravity on the brain causes the wisps of dreams to evaporate the moment you move.

Before you sit up or reach for the pen, replay the dream in your mind several times to make sure you have it.
Give it a title. This is not the place to get creative. You're not going for a Pulitzer, just a title that conveys the essence of the dream and thereby helps you hold on to it.

Catch whatever is in your mind when you awake.
If you don't have a dream, note what thoughts or phrases or musical tunes are running through your head when you wake up. Note, too, how you feel emotionally. They can be clues to the dreams you had before waking. Record whatever you have.

Record the dream in present tense.

If you want to work with the dream as more than material for your creative work, ask yourself how the dream makes you feel, and note it. Then ask if the dream could play out in your waking life. Dreams are often prophetic, giving you a heads up on what may happen. I once did dreamwork with someone who dreamed of someone who appeared to be her future editor, but didn't discover that's who the woman in her dream was until a few years later, when she'd finished a manuscript about her experiences healing through dreaming. Through the referral of an author friend, the woman in her dream became her editor for that manuscript.

If the events of the dream are too, well, dreamlike and not likely to happen in your waking reality, look at the dream's story line, and any symbols, metaphors, or word play contained in it. Dreams often use puns both in images and words. Consider your dream a message. Sometimes it might be for your personal life, but just as often it could be for your creative work. Same thing from any tunes, images, or phrases that were running through your head.

Create a space in the back of your journal to record animals, symbols, colors, places, or people that seem to have a special resonance for you, especially creatively.

If you aren't sure of their significance, use a symbol dictionary or other references to explore meanings. I usually advise against using a dream dictionary, because people tend to read the one or two meanings in the dictionary and assume that's what that animal or color or other element means. On the contrary, we each have our own dream language. For instance, a snake in your dream may be scary, while to someone else (like me) and depending on how it looks, the snake would be a welcome sign or symbol of some energy being activated in their life. Also record your emotional responses or associations to that element. The pages at the back of your journal (or in a separate journal) become your personal dream dictionary or creative collection filled with images, conflicts, colors, and more.

To use the dream for creative fuel, go back through the dream and underline any words, phrases or images that you respond to strongly. For instance, I had a dream that seemed to take place long, long ago and featured vultures. After recording the dream, I noted that the images of the dream—a drought, a woman unafraid of the vultures, and the vultures themselves—seemed to beg a story. The dream inspired my novel, *In the Land of the Vultures.*

Recording and working with the dream does not need to be limited to words. Don't hesitate to get out pencils and paints, or to print images off the internet (for your personal use only), or, if you happen to have old magazines or catalogs, use cuttings from those to illustrate the images and characters of the dream. Sometimes, working visually with the dream will help you recall more or catch more details than only writing the dream down, or lead to new ideas.

What if you are in the middle of a creative project and don't know where to go next with it?

TO INCUBATE A DREAM

To incubate a dream, as mentioned previously, clarify what you want to know about your project. What needs to be answered for you to move forward with ease again? As with any oracle, the more specific your question, the more likely you are to get a specific answer. Of course, there is nothing wrong with writing down, "Please tell me what I most need to know about this project."

Because it is more general, when you have a dream you might have to let it percolate for a while before you are able to harvest all the information you need from it.

When you incubate a dream, as with inspiration and creativity, do not try to control the process too much, or the outcome. When I am teaching, I always warn students not to insist the dream show up that night, the next night, or even the next. Be patient with the process. Try it one or two nights, take a break, and then try it again. Also, an important caveat here: do not decide that the dream that came to you the night you incubated one is not the dream you asked for. Again, even as creatives, we naturally expect things to go a certain way, and when the dream appears to be a nonsense about clowns and big red balloons when we were asking about a murder scene, that doesn't mean the dream isn't about that scene. It may be that we aren't seeing what is being offered.

A dream, like a lotus, has many petals or layers to it, and all the layers are seldom revealed at once. Live with the dream that shows up. Think about it. Look for puns, both visual and verbal. Look at colors, words, characters, emotion, actions. Each dream is a rich tapestry woven of many threads.

But what if you've tried everything above and still aren't remembering any dreams? That's when conscious dreamwork comes to the rescue.

Conscious dreamwork is done while you are . . . conscious. That is, you are not asleep, but your brain is, one hopes, in a theta state, usually arrived at with the use of the repetitive, rhythmic beat of a frame drum. The theta state is the liminal place for the brain between waking and sleeping, between the conscious and subconscious worlds. It occurs in hypnosis and REM sleep and is the state for deep learning, healing, and growth.

Your first step in the process is, as with an incubated sleep dream, to identify what your intent is. For instance, you may decide to visit a dream library, spend time with a mentor asking questions about your current creative project, or ask what is getting in your way to completing it. Write down your intent in your journal.

It's helpful when doing conscious dreamwork to start from a place such as a favorite tree—or tower—real or imagined. In shamanic work, you can use the tree as a gateway either into the underworld by descending through the roots, or into this reality via the lower branches, or into the upper world with the topmost branches. The upper world is usually where you want to travel when you want to speak with spirits. The middle world is this reality and is where you travel in order to see, know, or communicate with things or people in this reality that are at a distance. The underworld is where you go in order to work with animal guides, and other beings and places deep in the unconscious.

Before you begin a conscious dream journey, make sure that your space is protected and you won't be interrupted. Then get comfortable in a soft chair or sofa or lie down, either on a bed or on a floor with a rug or mat. Close your eyes. Let your body relax and your breathing deepen. If, like I do, you have a frame drum, then you can drum while you journey. Otherwise, play a recording of shamanic or trance drumming. Earphones are best here.

Imagine your tree. Imagine yourself opening a door into your tree and traveling down the steps inside until you emerge from the tree into another world.

With your intent or question clearly in mind, allow the experience to unfold before you. An animal may come to greet you. You may find yourself in a space different from where you live. See what or whom will speak to you. If you feel you are getting off track, just wandering, repeat your intent or question and continue. As with sleep dreams, there is a delicate balance between keeping a clear intent and controlling the experience too much, so keep your intent clear and trust your instincts. Trust your instincts, too, when it comes to what is happening. If it doesn't feel right, restate your purpose and move on, or, if you feel uncomfortable, retrace your steps and return back to yourself. Otherwise, enjoy the journey. When you have enough guidance or information or feel a need to return, retrace your steps to your tree, climb the stairs, and come back into your body. Give yourself a few moments to become fully present and then record the dream experience as you would a sleep dream.

I've taught dream workshops where a participant or two will not experience or "get" anything during the drumming. Don't worry, especially if you are new to the experience. It may be that you just need to get used to the process. Or that you needed to rest instead of travel. Again, let the experience be what it is. If you have any feelings, heard any sounds, or saw anything, record that.

Finally, if you are having challenges with both of these dream experiences, then you might want to try working with oracle cards, especially the Tarot. I think of the

Tarot as a conscious dream. Using the cards allows you to tune into the more instinctive and intuitive sides of yourself. When working with creative groups and teaching them to do dreamwork, I often include Tarot in the process because the cards can be helpful in understanding a dream. They are also an effective gateway into a conscious dream. And they can be the dream experience itself.

I'll show you how to use the rich and magical material of your dreams, both sleeping and conscious, in the next chapter. For now, get used to recording and playing with your dreams. Try a short conscious dream with a clear question or intention in mind.

Sleeping Beauty was sleeping, but that sleep rewarded her with many experiences and rich material for her life.

Journal Work

Make a list of any questions you have about your current project. If you are writing a novel, you might want to know how to get your character out of a situation. If you are composing a musical piece, you might ask how to deepen the mood or create more excitement. If you are filming a video, how to best frame an important scene or shot.

Ritual Work

Create a short ritual to protect your dream space, especially your conscious dream space. Turning off your phone might be part of it (or at least silencing it). You don't want to be jarred out of the dream journey.

Dreamwork

Write your project question down on a piece of paper. Then either "sleep on it" literally by putting it under your pillow before you go to sleep, or use it as the focus for a conscious dream journey. If this is your first journey, make it simple and short.

USING THE DREAM MAGIC

She picked up the feather, and when the owl hooted at her, she followed it into the deep shadows of the woods, unafraid and truly awake.

In his book *The Secret History of Dreaming*, Robert Moss writes, "One of the first uses of writing—which was invented in Sumer—was to record dreams, and that one of the great things that emerged from recording dreams—at least five thousand years ago—was literature. Writers have *always* been dreamers."

Indeed, Naomi Epel proved that truth with her book *Writers Dreaming*, published in 1993. In it, she shares the stories of such literary and popular writers as Isabel Allende, Stephen King, William Styron, Maya Angelou, and more, all of whom credit dreams with the inspirations for stories and for the creative process. Angelou talks about the dream of tall buildings being constructed as a sign her writing is going well. Styron, working on a novel, had such a powerful and moving dream that he abandoned his then-current project to work on the book that became *Sophie's Choice*. If Styron had been a painter instead of a writer, the dream image might have prompted a portrait conveying the mood of the woman, and the significance of that tattoo. Or, if a sculptor, would he have done a bust of her with her arm out and the number deeply etched there?

But lest you think only writers have been inspired by dreams, here's a wonderful quote from John Lennon: "The best songs are the ones that come to you in the middle of the night, and you have to get up and write them down, so you can go back to sleep."

For several years, I consulted on the dreams of country music stars for *People Magazine: Country Edition*. I provided dream insights and understandings for numerous country musicians, including Blake Shelton, Chris Young, Kimberly Schlapman, Miranda Lambert, and more. But it was the first dream from Rodney Atkins that remains one of my favorites.

"I have had a dream that I run into Loretta Lynn at McDonald's, and she sings me a song and I get a napkin to write it down on, and she sings it again." When he wakes during the night, he assumes he doesn't have to write it down because he already did . . . on the napkin. But then he wakes up in the morning and he wonders, "Where's my freaking napkin?"

For me, that was a perfect example of the Muse visiting in a dream in the guise of Loretta Lynn. My response to the dream as published in the magazine was "It's interesting that it takes place at McDonald's. It speaks to who he is—everyday people. Loretta perhaps represents his desire to achieve her level of long-term success. And he should be keeping a journal and pen by his bed because this could be a big song!"

His dream was also the perfect example of what happens when we don't pay attention to our dreams and don't take the time to record them. We often lose the inspiration and the potential project. Imagine how that makes your Muse feel.

Painters have also been inspired by dreams and used the dreams as the source of images for their work. William Blake's writing and paintings were inspired by dreams. Surrealists such as Salvador Dalí, Joan Miró, and others were drawn by that superior reality of dreams, and the images, colors, and distorted perspectives reflected that.

Because we are all dreamers, it is no surprise that dreams inspire creative work, just as they affect and influence other aspects of life. The key, though, is to first pay attention to your dreams, and then to respect and honor their gifts.

In addition to providing information on your life and serving as your dream dictionary, your dream journal also provides you with an unending source of material to work from.

NARRATIVE IDEA

A writer's most common use of dreams is as the initial creative impulse for story, plot, or character. In that story about William Styron, from *Writers Dreaming*, Epel writes about Styron's dream of "a woman he had known in his early twenties. He could see her standing in a hallway, her arms full of books, the blue numbers of a tattoo visible beneath her sleeve." That's the image that prompted him to turn his attention from his previous project to working on *Sophie's Choice*. He wrote the opening paragraph directly after the dream. Notice that it wasn't the action of a dream but rather the clarity of the image that stirred his imagination.

If you have a dream that seems more like someone else's story rather than your own, consider that it might be grist for your creative mill.

MOOD AND METAPHOR

If you want to use a particular dream for metaphor or mood, go back through the dream and underline any words or phrases that you respond to strongly, or any images that strike your fancy. For instance, I had a dream of a tree silhouetted against a night sky, and in the tree were eight screech owls! I might use that image as a particularly potent setting for a scene in a fantasy or murder mystery, or as an image for a music video to convey a feeling of warning or foreboding.

VERY IMPORTANT DREAM PEOPLE (VIDPS)

Have you used your observations of people on a plane or in the coffee shop or at the theater as ideas for your creative work? If so, then you can do the same with the people who show up in your dreams.

When dream characters demand your attention or make you curious, first record their name. If you have no name, then give the character a name according to her role in the dream; for example, "mother," "scary old man," or "benevolent guide." Write a description of the character, or draw them, including their clothing and any other interesting detail. Does the person remind you of someone from waking reality? Is there something about this person's character that plays into your current project? Or, like Styron's *Sophie*, something that gives you an idea for a new work?

Is the dream character a messenger with inspiration or information for you, or a performer, someone you can expand on in your work? If you dialogue with the character, in the dream or in your journal, what do they have to say to you?

DREAMSCAPES

How many times have you had a dream where the setting looks like no place you've ever been before? How many of those dreamscapes would make a wonderful setting for a story or a great painting, even if you used only the colors? Or what about that fantastic building could you incorporate into your design of a new office or residence?

If you want to make the most of a dreamscape, record the setting, describing it in as much detail as possible. Does this place have a name? A time period? Is this place found in waking reality; for example, Pittsburgh? Or is it in another realm such as Sleeping Beauty's castle protected by a hedge? Are there people in this dreamscape, and, if so, what are they doing? What emotion does this place evoke? Why?

Dreamscapes are fun to draw or paint or collage. Often there is an element of the absurd or impossible in them. What fun to explore that and extrapolate from it.

CHARACTER'S DREAMS

If you are a writer, screenwriter, or playwright, your recorded dreams can serve as dreams for your own characters when they experience challenges or opportunities such as relationships, changes in career, or illness. Using your dreams or modifying them to suit the story will give the character's dream sequence a ring of truth—and originality.

Even with all this dream material, what can you do if you feel blocked or uncertain about the next direction or steps for your creative project?

Well, you can always, as discussed previously, **incubate a dream**. In addition to asking project questions, ask about the best place to exhibit, or the agents to approach or for a title. Or you can ask for a dream to open the door to your own creative power.

Dream Forward

Dream a creative project forward. Waking from a half-finished dream is not unusual, but it can be frustrating. Kind of like getting to the middle of a movie and having the playback device shut down. Fortunately, there's a dream technique for moving both the dream and your project forward. You can do this in a conscious dream with the aid of a recording of drumming, or you can do this as you fall asleep.

The key is to focus on a primary or emotionally strong place or element of the dream or the project. Also, focus on your desire to see what comes next.

Get yourself comfortable on a bed or chair, lay your head back, and close your eyes. Then imagine that place in the dream or the element of your work where you want to find out "What happens next?" For the dream, see the print of the paper on the walls, the texture of the carpet. If you are outside, note the weather, the season, and the geography. Imagine it as clearly as possible. Then, with your project and question in mind, see yourself stepping into the dream.

Staying relaxed, ask "What next?" and allow the dream to unfold. Is there a forward motion to the dream, a sense of plotline developing? Does the environment around you change, suggesting a change in setting or mood? If someone else shows up in the dream, take the opportunity to dialogue with them. Ask them if they know "What next?" Return and record your experience—with words or images or even music—using the techniques for recording a dream.

Visiting Your Dream Library, Museum, or Performance Space

A third fun technique for moving over, under, or around creative blocks is a dream journey, I learned from Robert Moss: visiting your dream library. A library like no other, it's meant solely for your research, for your visits with creative mentors, and to discover work not yet put out into the world. I've shared this dream journey with many writers, who always enjoy it.

If you create in a form that normally wouldn't be found in a library, then consider a dream museum, gallery, or performance space. It is your ideal dream space, after all. Taking a conscious dream journey to this library or other ideal space can, at the minimum, be fun and even relaxing. At its best, though, a journey to your dream library can provide answers to questions and give you a strong affirmation of your work. And I know this technique works from personal experience and the experience of students.

As with the dream reentry, get yourself in a relaxed state and, using either relaxing soft music or drumming, see in your mind that special library or space. It could be a library in waking reality, such as one from your childhood, perhaps the Bookmobile, or it could be totally imagined, such as one in a large room with high ceilings and leaded-glass windows—and one of those ladders that moves on wheels among the walls of books.

Define your intention. Do you want to find some specific information on food in the eighteenth century? Or do you want to meet a mentor such as Ernest Hemingway or Chopin? Do you want to see your own yet-to-be-born book so that you can see its title or discover who will buy your movie trailer music?

As you enter the library or other space, see it clearly—its furnishings, the art on the walls, the scenes outside the windows, other people. Follow your instincts as you search for information or talk to people there. If you are looking for your own book, where would it be shelved? Go there. When you find it, take it out, examine the cover, open it, and look at the contents. Read some of the text or the acknowledgments (you might find the name of your agent and editor there!).

Perhaps you want to study the artwork hanging on the walls. Is it yours? Is there a frame around a canvas you have yet to paint? Whatever your medium, search for what you are looking for in your ideal dream library. Spend as much time as you like.

When you are ready, return from your journey and record everything you have seen and experienced. Then follow through by checking out any information you were given.

These techniques of dream incubation, reentry, and visiting your dream library are effective tools for creating and moving through blocks, whatever your medium or form of expression. The only limitation is your imagination and your willingness to play. If you tell yourself it won't work, it won't.

But if you dive into the dreamworld with the same enthusiasm you have when you dive into your creative work, you will discover a place of infinite inspiration, information, and support.

Journal Work

What would you like to know about the direction of your current project, the "What next?"? If you could talk to someone in your field from the past, who would it be? Why?

Ritual Work

After any recent dreamwork, or the dreamwork that follows, choose an action to honor the dream, such as read a book on the subject, draw a picture of a scene in the dream, or listen to music that is appropriate to the dream. And give thanks to the dream messengers . . . maybe with something to drink or a sweet treat.

Dreamwork

Clarify and simplify your question from the journal work above. Then incubate a dream, dream a dream or the work forward, or visit your dream library to find answers to your question. Be sure to record your experience. Answers may not be immediately apparent, but recording the dream means you can return to it and look at it from different perspectives.

PART THREE

THE PRINCE

TESTING TIME AND REALITY

Every year, the hedge of thorns grew higher and higher until at last it enclosed the castle in its branches of thorns, even over the top of the castle, so that nothing could be seen of it, not even the flag upon the roof. But, in spite of the castle not being visible from the road, the story of the beautiful sleeping princess circulated from hearth to hearth around the countryside and beyond, so that princes from other realms came and tried to get through the thorny barrier. Indeed, it was as if the thorny hedge were a fierce warrior battling each adventurous prince, refusing them entrance and, instead, catching them up on the sword-like thorns, holding fast to them until their ambitions and lives expired there.

All those poor princes impaled on those merciless thorns. No one to rescue them.

Worse, in spite of those bodies hanging lifelessly, yet one prince after another decides he will brave the hedge and waken the princess of the legend (because after almost one hundred years, any story becomes a legend). Each of those princes was blocked from their goal because of their insistence on forcing their way through the thorns on their timeline.

Can't you just hear each of them? "One hundred years? That's like . . . forever. How long has it been? No one knows. I could be dead by the time one hundred years has passed. I'm not waiting."

And so each one acts on their timeline. Not the story's. And isn't that interesting? After all, only one prince needed to show up at the right time. Why does the story have so many others sacrificing themselves in the misguided attempt to rush the timing?

Because timing is key to the story. The time had to be right; Briar Rose had to be the right age to prick her finger. She couldn't be fourteen or sixteen for the spell to work. She had to be fifteen years old. The spell couldn't be broken at fifty years or ninety years; it had to be one hundred years.

And just as with the story, timing is critical in the creative process. And so is patience.

For the prince, it's possible synchronicity plays a part. Synchronicity, a concept first introduced by psychologist Carl Jung, is the simultaneous occurrence of events that appear to be significantly related but have no discernible causal relationship. In the story, is the prince just one more in a line of princes, or is he the right prince at the right time? What brings him to the thorny hedge at that particular moment? A commanding father who is king and wants this realm annexed to his own? A chance tale told over ales at the local pub where the prince stopped on his travels? A Wise Woman whispering in his ear as he sleeps at night (i.e., his own dream)? How did he arrive at just the right time?

Arriving at the "right time" on a creative project or in your career is always a challenge, isn't it? After all, no one tells you that the spell on you and your work that keeps you from completing or launching into the world will last only three years or one hundred days. Even beginning a journey into your creative work may have all been happenstance.

I wanted to be a writer and published author since I wrote and illustrated my first book around the age of seven ("The Thin Man and the Fat Man"). In college, I majored in creative writing / English and took all the courses that would move me toward being a professional writer. Even after I was married and working full time, I wrote stories and tried to get published. The closest I came for years was publishing articles in the in-house magazine of the company I worked for. Years later, I enrolled in a master's degree course. My thesis requirement for the degree was a one-person exhibit of my framed weavings and the manuscript of a young-adult fantasy novel. After my degree, I polished the manuscript and sent it out on submission and received rejections. I didn't continue to submit because, with three young sons, followed by a growing weaving business, my writing fell lower on my priority list. I published articles, but no book. The timing didn't seem to be right, and I had no idea when it would be. Could I have forced the issue? Probably. But with everything else going on in my life, I probably would have ended up as a skeleton on the thorns.

Then, in March 2000, I stood in my booth filled with my colorful scarves and shawls and jackets at a craft show in Virginia, and a woman walked in to look at the work. We engaged in conversation, and when she found out I was a writer, she told me she was the emcee for the Maui Writers Conference, a conference I had dreamed of attending for years. But the cost! The woman urged me to come to the conference, to apply as a speaker host, and to use her as a referral. Never in my wildest dreams—and some of them get pretty wild—did I imagine that a conference I wanted to attend in

Hawaii would manifest in a booth in Virginia. Synchronicity? Magic?

The spell was broken somewhat. I didn't sign with an agent or editor, but I was suddenly exposed to many of them. Speaking with them, introducing them, and helping other writers get their pitches honed. At least I wasn't impaled on a thorn. And I thought more seriously of myself as a writer.

The following year, I again worked at the conference and had a chance to pitch to an agent who didn't like the project I was pitching her (this project, actually, with a slightly different focus). She asked if I had thought of writing a book using weaving as a metaphor. In fact, I had. Surely, now the spell was broken?

Not quite, because even though I signed on with the agent and she did three rounds of submissions and I had interest from a major publisher, in the end the book didn't sell. The agent, discouraged, let me go, suggesting I consider self-publishing, still not a popular alternative at that point in time, before e-publishing and e-readers.

Nevertheless, I did self-publish, and the book, *Weaving a Woman's Life: Spiritual Lessons from the Loom*, won awards and is still selling.

What is really interesting to me about the spell, though, is that the book you hold in your hands, though a different version of what I originally intended, is the book I originally pitched to that editor in Maui years ago.

The timing wasn't right then. But after meeting a representative of Schiffer years ago at another conference—not for writers but for Tarot readers, the right time is now. Apparently, the hundred years is up. The thorns parted for me. I just had to be patient.

Patience is a hard discipline to practice for creatives. Not because you don't have it, but because it is often tested to its limits. Almost twenty years is a long time to wait for a project to come to fruition. Whatever your number of years or rejections or exhibits or performances, patience is pulled thin.

No wonder, then, that sometimes creatives rush projects and products into the world before they are ready. The digital age, with its ability to produce and distribute quickly with minimal gatekeepers (threshold guardians), makes it easy to charge ahead. The act of rushing work into the world is what Professor Richard Restak, in a Great Courses lecture about creativity, calls premature closure, which is "reaching a conclusion or accepting an explanation before examining the facts and the logical conclusions flowing from these facts." He states that premature closure is a result of discomfort with functioning in the midst of ambiguity and uncertainty—a resistance to not having answers to questions.

Certainly, none of those princes approaching the hedge had an answer to the question of whether or not they could make it through. Just as we don't usually have answers to the questions of success or failure in our work, questions such as "Can I do this? Will someone like it? Like it enough to publish it, buy it, exhibit it, have it performed?" The lack of answers, the ambiguity, and the uncertainty are uncomfortable and why some creatives abandon projects midway, beginning work on new projects that seem easier and more exciting. The discomfort with lack of answers also triggers that R word . . . Resistance.

Steven Pressfield, in his book *The War of Art*, writes extensively about the role of resistance and its most common manifestation in our creative work, procrastination. And in Restak's lecture on creativity, it becomes obvious that one of the major sources for that resistance is that you want answers! You resist ambiguity and uncertainty—even though, ironically, an ability to function with ambiguity and uncertainty is an identifying characteristic of creativity.

After all, how many times have you wanted to know exactly what the next scene in your novel should be, or what the best color is to add depth to that rose glaze, or even whether or not to self-publish that score you just composed? Those unanswered questions and many more are lived with every day, first because we are all human, and second because we are striving to be at our optimal creative best.

Think about the uncertainties you face every day in your creative work. Then add the uncertainties of everyday life.

Premature closure is one of your defenses in the midst of all that uncertainty. For creatives, it isn't a matter of arriving at a conclusion before examining all the facts. Instead, it is reaching an assumed and early conclusion to the work in order to leave uncertainty and ambiguity behind. Disappointingly, the push for conclusion too often lacks originality, integrity, or vision. In the midst of discomfort or unhappiness, it feels easier to push to conclusion by using tried-and-true forms or formats from the past, or simplified or superficial direction or solutions, or imitative work.

It is easier to travel a familiar path through uncertain territory than it is to choose a new path and therefore more ambiguity. Premature closure may lead to quitting, pushing forward too soon and too fast to launch the work, or giving up instead of reevaluating the work or the approach to marketing it. Just look at those impaled princes.

The other side of this, however, is the unwillingness to show up at all, or the dillydallying at making the attempt. The spell is never going to be broken if no one braves the hedge of thorns. Scary as it might be.

Waiting for the perfect moment, waiting until the project is perfect, is only another way to avoid the ambiguity. As mentioned above, Pressfield calls procrastination the most common manifestation of resistance because it's the easiest to rationalize. He writes, "We don't tell ourselves, 'I'm never going to write my symphony.' Instead we say, 'I am going to write my symphony; I'm just going to start tomorrow.'"

I certainly know that experience; do you? Whether working on a novel or this book, it was easier to think, "I'll work on it later," than to sit down and deal with the ambiguity of what to write next.

Because, of course, you want the work to be perfect. To be sensational and beautiful and awe-inspiring. You want to be the heroic creative, slashing through the thorns to arrive at the castle and save the Princess.

But those thorns.

And yet, time doesn't stop, though you wish it did. It keeps moving forward, tick tock. And you can hear it, those seconds, and minutes, and hours, ticking away. And if you wait too long, will the opportunity to brave those thorns and kiss the Princess slip away?

What if the Prince had waited one day, one month, or one year longer? What then?

What if the Prince was too busy that day? Figured he'd get to that thorny problem tomorrow?

Too frequently over the years, I've watched clients who come to me for creativity or book coaching fail to finish or, once finished, fail to submit the work to be juried, agented, or auditioned. The reasons always sound . . . reasonable. But there are reasons below the reasons that have to do with fear. Fear of rejection and criticism, not just by others in the creative field but by friends and family. And time keeps moving on. The opportunity to move through that thorny hedge is lost.

Like the Prince, you have to decide whether you believe in the legend or dream enough to move forward and take the risk. Is now the time for you? Are you ready to get off the horse, take sword in hand, and step forward, ready for whatever comes next?

Journal Work

When in the past did you miss an opportunity for you or your creative work to move forward? When was your timing synchronous and magical? What resulted in both cases?

Ritual Work

Find a small clock or a picture of one (an analog clock, not a digital clock) that you can put on your creativity altar, or in a special place. Light a candle. Take a few deep breaths to center yourself. You and the clock and time have a lot in common. Just as the clock tick-tocks the second, you breathe in and out. Your heart beats, pulsing blood throughout your body. Tick tock. The blood circulates; that is, it takes a circular path out from and back to the heart. The hands on the clock move in a circle too. Breathe with time, counting in and out. You are part of time. Time is part of you. You tap into time to move with it, not against it. Breathe in and out. When you've really felt yourself part of time, in time with time, then inhale, hold, and breathe out. Blow out the candle. For a day or a week, be mindful of time, timing, and your compatibility with it.

For this, you probably want to do a conscious dream. After you are comfortable, imagine yourself standing next to a steadily moving stream. It's not a deep stream. No higher than the tops of your legs, so you don't have to be afraid to wade in. The water is almost body temperature. A little cool but not cold. This is the River of Time.

Stand facing against the current. Look upstream. Everything flows toward you. Take a few steps and feel the push of the water against your legs; notice how you have to be determined to move forward against the current. If you keep walking, how long will it be before you tire? Before the muscles of your legs start to ache?

Now turn around and face downstream. Feel the water pushing against the back of your legs. Take a step. Then another. No fighting. No struggle.

Is what you desire for yourself and your work upstream or downstream? Are you trying to reach an opportunity such as an exhibit or performance that is a ways upstream? Or one that passed by and is already around the curve downstream?

What are you willing to do to reach your desire? Is there someone standing on the banks who sees your desire and you at the same time? Can you ask them for suggestions or guidance on whether to proceed in one direction or another?

What is your body telling you as you stand there? Do you need to move or be still? Do you need to be part of the stream but not moved by it?

When you have some answers, or you've explored the experience enough, step out of the stream, returning to dry ground. Feel your feet firmly planted. Bring your awareness back to the present and your place. Slowly open your eyes.

Make notes of your experience and any information you received.

STEPPING FORWARD
WITH CURIOSITY, COURAGE,
AND COMMITMENT

Having heard the story of the Sleeping Beauty while traveling about his father's realm, the Prince decided to investigate the story himself. Asking one person after another about the story and where the castle might be, he finally arrived at a threatening-looking thicket where an old man sat on the ground with his dog, whittling on a bit of wood in his hands, while puffing on a pipe. "Grandfather," said the Prince, "is this the place of the Sleeping Princess?" Being a man of few words, the old man answered, "Aye, 'tis. But be ye sure you want to dare this hedge? Some mighty sharp thorns be there. Many have tried and died." The Prince looked up at the hedge and swallowed. "But is it not true that a hundred years has passed?" The old man nodded and reached out to pat his dog, who lay panting in the shade. "Aye, 'tis. But only a Prince can rescue the Sleeping Princess. Be you a Prince?" The Prince nodded, and with thoughts of love and glory, he threw his shoulders back and lifted the sword in his hand.

Creating requires courage and commitment. The root of courage comes from the Latin *cor*, meaning heart, having to do with valor and the quality of mind that enables one to meet danger or trouble.

Usually, courage is associated with the metaphor of having the heart of a lion; hence, Richard I, who was famous for his military campaigns and defense of France, was called Richard Coeur de Lion or Richard Lionheart.

Ironically, Frank Baum, in his first book about the land of Oz, created a character known as the Cowardly Lion, the very opposite of what is usually associated with the lion. Baum's character seeks out the Wizard, hoping the ultimate magician will be able to give him the courage he so lacks. The Wizard tells the lion that anyone can have courage, and his gift to him was a medal awarded for meritorious conduct and bravery against witches. What is interesting about the Wizard's gift to the lion is that it doesn't bestow bravery but *recognition* for bravery already exhibited.

It's easy to forget that as a creative, you exhibit bravery every time you begin a new work, continue to create the work, and then put the work out in the world. And yet, for many, approaching that blank canvas or page or that lump of clay or molten glass triggers trembling knees and a fast-beating heart. Is it any wonder that some creatives frame their first check (as in the old days) or the first email from PayPal reporting that they have money from a sale? That is the creative's medal for bravery.

Courage is as necessary for creatives as curiosity, perhaps more so.

The story of Sleeping Beauty would never unfold without a heroine curious enough to explore her world, climb that tower, and reach out to that spindle.

And the story would never arrive at its happy conclusion if the Prince didn't have the courage to brave the thorns of the hedge.

The forest or woods show up often in fairy tales as a place of the unknown and where danger abides. Think of "Goldilocks and the Three Bears," "Hansel and Gretel," "Snow White and the Seven Dwarfs," and many more. And though danger lurks in the shadows of the forest, transformation is the gift.

In the tale of Sleeping Beauty, the hedge takes the role of the forest, being both a place of danger and transformation. It is also the bridge between the outer world of other realms and people going about their daily lives and the inner world of the castle and its inhabitants, including Briar Rose. The Prince, as he steps into the hedge, is aware that everything after this moment will never be the same. Either he'll end up as the other challengers have, a skeleton hanging from the thorns befitting a Halloween display, or he'll do what no one else has succeeded in doing—entering the castle, finding the Sleeping Beauty, and kissing her awake. In either case, he'll no longer be the adventuring bachelor.

In different versions of the fairy tale, an old man (the male version of the Wise Woman in the tower?) sits outside the hedge, warning all the adventurers of the conditions for entering the hedge. You must not only be brave, but you must also be a Prince.

But why a Prince?

The answer to this question is very much a challenge for creatives.

In the time of the tale, and still in places around the world, a royal would not deign to marry a commoner, someone not of royal or noble blood or birth. Therefore, the twelfth fairy or Wise Woman would not make anyone but a Prince the rescuer of Briar Rose from her long sleep. After all, his task is to kiss her awake. And, if successful, he will be awarded her hand in marriage. So it couldn't be a farmer or a baker. Her rescuer must be of royal or noble birth.

He must be worthy.

Worthy.

Do you feel the energy around that word? How it resonates for you as a creative?

Having worth or being worthy is having qualities or abilities that merit recognition in a certain way. In the fairy tale, royal blood along with courage and commitment are the qualities that signify the Prince's worthiness.

Briar Rose is worthy of the Prince because of her royal blood and her innocence. And perhaps, in the Prince's mind, she is worthy because she needs him to rescue her.

Creatives worry about worthiness too.

They worry, "Is this project worthy of my time and attention?" And, conversely, "Am I worthy of the inspiration and the project with its challenges?" And when the project is near completion, "Is it good enough, have I done enough, is it worthy of attention, exhibition, performance, and sales?"

Bottom line? Am I worth it? Is my work worth it?

The Prince believes in his worthiness because he is, after all, a prince. Has his courage and commitment been previously tested and proved worthy? We don't know. Perhaps, for him, being a Prince is all that is necessary. For you, perhaps knowing that you are a writer, or singer, or composer, or painter, or _____ is all that is necessary to deem you worthy.

As comfortable as Briar Rose may be in her soft bed dreaming her dreams, she's not meant to lie there forever. It's her bed. Not her bier.

And your creative ideas are not meant to lie sleeping in your mind and imagination forever. Former Pittsburgh composer Billy May, who scored music for television and film, said that you have a hundred creative horses. Are you going to give them their heads and let them run the race, or will you take them back to the stable to keep them safe—because you are afraid they aren't good enough to compete?

If the Prince never takes action, doesn't believe he is worthy of the call, and lacks courage and commitment to dare the hedge, not only will he never reap the rewards awaiting him, but the castle and all its sleeping inhabitants will never rejoin the world.

And what a loss that would be, not just to the Prince and Princess, but to both their realms as well.

The Prince must believe he is worthy. He must take his heart in his hands and have the courage to venture forth, but he must also make the commitment to the journey.

When you commit, you not only choose a course of action but you dedicate or pledge yourself to it, as with the "I do" of a marriage vow.

Sleeping Beauty has not committed or dedicated herself to anything yet. She's been put under a spell, and yes, she is actively dreaming and imagining, open to the realm of creative possibilities, but no commitment or vow has yet been expressed.

The Prince stands at the beginning of the hedge and has yet made no commitment either.

Creativity requires, along with curiosity and courage, commitment.

Sometimes, like the Prince, when you commit to something, such as a relationship, a job, or writing a book, you do so with the naiveté of the untried and the untested. You commit with optimism and hope, and with that belief in happy endings.

Then you experience the work that the commitment requires. The true grit. The "getting up every day and working at it no matter what" true grit that a job, a relationship, or your creative work requires. Courage for seeing the project through may weaken, and questions arise. "Is this really that important? Is this really what I want? WHY AM I DOING THIS?"

Whatever the reason, without a commitment it is too easy to give up and turn back. A malaise of modern times is the commitment that is really no commitment: "I'll do this as long as I enjoy it or until it gets hard."

Commitment is a scary thing. If your songs, your paintings, your novels, or your weavings are to have life, find a home, and grow into the fullness of their potential, you must commit to giving them your love and your respect without reserve—and often without reward.

The challenge, of course, is to keep saying, "I do" when you are tired, short tempered, and frustrated, to continue to love and honor your efforts to create what has meaning, beauty, and significance even in the face of criticism or failure or lack of funds.

What if the Prince's commitment was "Yeah, I'll do this, but if those thorns are the least bit threatening, then I'm outta here"? Then it would be "Too bad, Sleeping Beauty." The imagined creations, the dreams she dreamed, would be left to languish and die on those thorns right along with the failed attempts of the other men.

Moving your work from idea to actual product, and then moving it into the world for acceptance or rejection, is breath stopping, stomach churning, sweat inducing, and just plain scary. Ask any debut artist exhibiting for the first time. Or ask any novelist launching her thirtieth book.

Frightening. Absolutely frightening.

But creativity is sacred, and you are called to give it everything you have.

Something in your heart and soul longs for the adventurous journey of the commitment and for the satisfaction of fulfilling it, for the happily ever after.

So, you need to commit. Take your sword, of course. More importantly, take your heart in your hands and bravely say, "I do."

Journal Work

Have you committed to your creativity? If so, is your commitment conditional? What are the conditions? Committed until it gets hard? Or you run out of money? Or you get a certain number of rejections? Fail to make sales after three months, six months? With past creative expressions or projects, did you stay committed or ask for a divorce? What is the commitment you are ready to make now?

Ritual Work

Remembering the parts of a ritual, design one for saying "I do," to your new or current project, to making the commitment you're ready to make. Write out the commitment that you place on your creativity altar as part of the ritual. Do the ritual at the New Moon.

Dreamwork

Incubate a dream asking to meet your project. Ask it what it needs from you and what are the signs or symbols showing how it is committed to you. Remember not to censor it or discount what shows up. If you have trouble incubating, try a conscious dream or use oracle cards.

BRAVING THE THORNS

Swallowing again, as much to convince himself as the old man, the Prince stepped forward toward the hedge, which was suddenly abloom with roses. And when he looked back to tell the old man of the roses, he saw that both man and dog were gone.

The Prince, armed with courage and commitment, steps past the old man (the threshold guardian), over the threshold into the hedge of thorns. He advances, braced for the worst, ready to do battle with those dangerous and deadly thorns, swallowing his fear as he passes one of the skeletons of a predecessor.

While you may not be a prince facing a hedge of thorns, you may feel very much like him when you face exposing your creative ideas, dreams, and products to others. Family and friends are risky enough, but putting your work in front of strangers? Some of them claiming the title of "critic"? Absolutely deadly!

In the Tarot, the oracle I use when coaching creatives, there is a card called Ten of Swords. On it, you see a man assailed by ten swords flying through the air at him, much as these hedge thorns probably seemed to fly at the hapless adventurer. In some decks, the man lies on the ground, with swords impaling him in the back. In the Tarot, the suit of swords is about the mind and everything connected to it, such as beliefs and attitudes and thoughts. Swords is also about communication, both internal and external. I always think that this card is a perfect illustration of a creative's feared experience of putting their work into the world. The thorns (i.e., the swords) seem to come at you from all directions.

And it isn't just one type of thorn that hangs you up. No, it's several different types.

YOUR OWN SELF-DOUBTS
AND FEARS

I've seen this repeatedly in clients and—let's be honest—on occasion in myself. When you aren't certain about whether or not your work measures up, is worthy (there's that word again), then one way to avoid having to face that thorn is to keep working on developing or polishing the work. You tell yourself it's not ready yet; you have to do one more thing. Except one more thing turns into a dozen more things, and the work is still in your space instead of in the world.

Or you launch the work but don't do everything you can to draw attention to it because you fear feedback and criticism. You don't send out announcements on social media. It's in the world, but you don't let the world know about it because you are flinching before thorns even touch you.

You use your imagination so well, coming up with all the ways your work will fail or be criticized, that there's no room for new ideas or possibilities. Expectations of what thorns you might face often hang you up and turn creative dreams to dust. Your imagination serves fear instead of serving your creativity, conjuring thorns to stab and destroy it.

OTHER PEOPLE'S FEARS, DOUBTS,
AND CRITICISMS

We don't just have to deal with the thorns of our own expectations though. The thorns that are often the most painful and debilitating, that feel like those swords in the back of that guy on the Tarot card, are the fears, doubts, and criticisms of family and friends. Those are the communications that leave us injured and immobilized, even though some of them are not meant to do that.

There are those well-meaning comments such as "That's a lovely idea for a story. Oh, by the way, did you check the ads for a job today?" Or "Well, that's just beautiful, but I wouldn't want to hang it over my sofa." Or "That's nice, dear, but where's the melody?" These and more comments are uttered for various reasons: to protect you, because they're too afraid to practice their own creativity and they don't like it when you do, or they don't know what else to say because they don't understand your work. And every comment cuts, some more deeply than others, depending on who says them and why, leaving you bleeding.

Then there are the rejections and critiques from agents, gallery owners, directors, conductors, and more. Those skeletons of failure, yours and others', hang in the hedge as horrific reminders of what happens when you dare to risk yourself and your creativity. This is where many creatives get . . . well, hung up. A few rejections, a few shows or exhibits that didn't sell well, and they shrug their shoulders and decide that the world isn't ready for their work, or that their work isn't good enough, so they go back to taking classes and creating new work but never do anything with it.

If you choose to create for your own joy and satisfaction, that's great. But don't choose it because you've experienced failure in the past and don't want to risk it again. Failure is part of life, from learning to walk to painting a masterpiece. Just think of those skeletons as Halloween decorations and keep moving. Don't let them or the thorns stop you from doing the work that calls to you.

Shakespeare said it best in Hamlet's famous "to be or not to be" soliloquy:

Whether 'tis nobler in the mind to suffer the slings and arrows of outrageous fortune,

Or to take arms against a sea of troubles, and by opposing end them.

In other words, obviously life is not lived solely in the happily-ever-after mode. In order to experience that, often it is necessary to suffer the slings and arrows . . . the thorns.

Disappointment, loss, fear, rejection, and betrayal are all part of life. They are also part of the creative life and process.

I don't believe in the idea that you have to suffer to create great art, and therefore you should go live in an unheated, barely furnished garret where you sit cold and miserable while you write the next Pulitzer-worthy novel or paint the next great masterpiece. That's not necessary.

We all suffer. One way or another, we all suffer loss and disappointment, fear and betrayal, rejection and criticism. The level of suffering is influenced by factors such as age, race, gender, economic status, and more, but we all suffer, no garret necessary. The level of suffering is not a factor in the development, depth, or success of the work, either. How you as a creative respond to your slings and arrows, the thorns of creativity, is one of the key factors to the significance and success of the work. How you express and develop your understanding and insights from your suffering and challenges is what makes the difference.

The hedge itself represents the barriers you erect so that you don't have to do the work. Note that the story doesn't share how many potential suitors and adventurers turned away from the hedge because it was too frightening or too much work to try to win the hand of a princess they may not even like. And if they saw any of the corpses or skeletons of previous attempts hanging from the hedge, really, wouldn't it be stupid to even try?

But . . .

What if the hedge wasn't even really there? What if everyone believed it was there because that's what the legend said—that a tall, deadly hedge had grown up around the castle—but the hedge existed solely in the imagination?

Because you see, hear, and experience only what you want or expect to see, hear, and experience.

For one hundred years, young men arrived at the spot where an old man sat, and believed the warning about the hedge. Because they believed in its thorns, that is what they experienced. They were motivated just enough to enter the hedge but had no vision for what lay beyond, just some illusory idea of a princess needing to be awakened. They had no concept of the castle she was in, the tower, or her. She could have aged. They didn't know. All they knew and believed in was the thorny hedge, so they expected a hard and painful, even deadly, experience. And that is what they got: hard, painful, and deadly.

How often has that happened to you? Other creatives who are doing work in your medium warn you about the slings and arrows of outrageous fortune that will assail you once you step foot on the path to bring the world to your work? Warnings such as "Don't be surprised if your work doesn't sell for a year. It takes awhile to build an audience." Or "Paranormal fiction isn't selling. Write something else." Or "Landscapes are so passé. Do you have any abstracts?" Or, as the rock group Queen heard about "Bohemian Rhapsody," "No one will listen to a song that is almost six minutes long."

Of course, the one thorn that hangs up many creatives, either through their own doubts or that of family members, is "You'll never make a living at this (or you'll never make any money). Be practical."

Your challenge is, as author and book coach Becca Syme, advises, "to question the premise."

Just because the old man says the hedge is deadly doesn't necessarily mean it is. Is the barrier—the currently unpopular fiction genre, the too-long score length, or the breaking-tradition art style—really there? And is it there for only some but not others? Perhaps you are the one who has waited until the right time and have the right style or qualifications to break the barrier, brave the hedge. After all, who are the ones telling you to beware and that you can't? And whose interest do they have at heart?

Question the premise and then be curious. What would happen if . . . ? Are you prepared? Do you have the knowledge, tools, and training necessary?

Perhaps the most important question of all is "How will I feel if I don't try? If I walk away? If I don't risk it?"

In the fairy tale, once the Prince decides to risk it all, brave the hedge, he steps forward. But instead of thorns, he is greeted with roses. Is it a matter of timing or perception, or both?

Historically, roses act as symbols for everything from the royal houses of England (such as the Stuarts) to being state flowers, to representing the Virgin Mary and Aphrodite, the latter the goddess of love.

In the language of flowers, a white rose represents purity and innocence. A pink rose represents appreciation and admiration. But it is the red rose that represents love and passion.

What do you imagine are the color or colors of the hedge roses? Are they pink, white, or red? Or perhaps they are a riot of color, promising the Prince purity, appreciation, and love?

Rose oil is used in cosmetics and perfumes, both because of its healing properties and because it is an aphrodisiac (from the goddess Aphrodite). So the scent of the roses is a soothing balm and an enticement to progress through the hedge, and a small reward for stepping forward.

When you commit to your creative project or process, there is a commitment of the heart to a sacred act: creativity. In some religious traditions, the rose represents the sacred or divine presence at work. For you, it is the presence of the Muse, there to remind you of your purpose and to give you her blessing. The roses also remind the Prince and you that if there is to be beauty and creativity in the world, you must step forward.

It is you who has the power to change thorns into roses, whether those thorns are your own self-doubts, or the criticisms of others, or the beliefs and tales from those who have come before.

You can transform that fearful hedge into a thing of sensory, expressive beauty.

Journal Work

What fears have you focused on and perhaps made bigger than they are? Have you let them hold you back? What would you create if there were no barriers, no dour words of "Impossible. Not done. Not popular."?

Ritual Work

If you can, buy yourself some roses for your creativity altar. They don't have to be the expensive ones. You don't have to buy a dozen, but purchase a few. Put them in a pleasing-to-your-eye container and set them on the altar. What color(s) did you choose? Breathe in any scent. Then, as you continue to breathe, close your eyes and imagine that some of the hedges and thorns standing between you and your creative goals are transforming. Because the time is right. Because you are willing to take a risk. Because you see your creative goal clearly. Breathe in and out until you feel the transformation of the thorns and skeletons of the hedge transform into blooming beauty. Give thanks. And remember to care for the roses until they have shed their petals.

Dreamwork

Look back through some of your recent dreams. Look for barriers that showed up. If not a hedge, a fence or stop sign or closed door. Anything that might represent something that stands in your way. How did you handle it in the dream? If you didn't or didn't do so successfully, try dream reentry, focusing on that barrier and asking what you need to do to remove or transform it.

ENTERING THE SILENCE—
AND THE CASTLE

In the castle yard, the Prince saw, through the open doors of the stable, that the horses slept, as did the hounds at the stall doors. On the stable roof, the pigeons slept with their heads under their wings. Not a bird was singing, not an insect buzzing. Quietly and carefully, the Prince trod the walkway to the castle doors. Hoping they weren't locked, the Prince pulled on the large iron ring, and the wooden door swung silently open, and he crossed over the threshold into the castle's kitchen, where the cook was slumped snoring over the kettle. Even the kitchen boy had fallen to the floor asleep with a chicken still in his grip, also asleep.

You know that old adage "Let sleeping dogs lie." The meaning of the proverb is that it is foolish to interfere in a situation that is currently causing no problems but might do so as a result of such interference. In the adage, you don't know how the dogs are going to react once you wake them. They could become agitated if they want to go for a walk or if they need to be fed. Or they could bite you in the butt.

But what could possibly go wrong with breaking a spell and waking a princess?

From the Prince's point of view, after dealing with that hedge, absolutely nothing. He's probably thinking, "I'll just lay one on her and we can all get to the partying and the happily ever after."

Except, it is never that simple, is it? Just when you've made it through the thorns of fear and doubt, rejection and criticism, there is silence. Crickets.

But no, not even crickets. Absolute silence. No birdsong, no voices, and nothing moves. Not even the leaves on the trees. Time and the pulse of life have stopped.

And the castle, this huge stone edifice, stolid and cold, only emphasizes that fact.

Here is the space between the idea and the reality. What was imagined and what is manifested in the world. Up to this point, Briar Rose has slept undisturbed, walking in dreams, and everyone is asleep with her. Time stopped for them, while beyond the hedge, time continued. And now, with the Prince, the timeless and the temporal meet. The Prince doesn't just bring the means of breaking the spell, he also brings the world with all its demands, expectations, and effects of time.

Here, between the hedge and the tower room, is "the pause that refreshes," an old advertising slogan of Coca-Cola back in 1929, a time just before the stock market crash, when people were feeling unsure but working hard. The campaign ads showed people from all walks of life pausing for a bottle of cola.

Things haven't become any less stressful since then, but silence and a pause that refreshes seem like an idea that has passed. Creatives especially are challenged to find time to rest, renew, and reconnect with the Muse and their creativity, because the creative work is something to be squeezed in among all the other demands of daily life. Nurturing the self is more a trend than a practice regularly observed.

Finding silence and solitude often feels like more trouble than they are worth.

In my book *Weaving a Woman's Life*, I devote a whole chapter to silence and solitude. At the beginning of the chapter, I quote Oriah Mountain Dreamer: "If there is one consistent thing that stops people committed to doing creative work from doing it, it is this: a lack of necessary silence in their lives, an inability or unwillingness to find and stay with the stillness, to regularly create empty time in their day or their week."

The pause that refreshes the creative mind and body, heart, and soul is helpful before looking for inspiration, during the creative work, after finishing the project, and before launching it into the world. It's also good any time that you feel soul weary or that your creative well has run dry.

It's one of the reasons that dreams are so healing and helpful—because they come to you when you are finally still . . . and silent.

Before the Prince can break the silence and his solitude, he has to first enter it. Does he stand just on the other side of the hedge, having successfully navigated it, and, encountering the stillness and silence, stand awestruck and a little afraid?

Silence and solitude are intimidating if you aren't used to them. Think of how they are used to punish prisoners: they are sent to solitary confinement. While it is meant to serve the safety of the rest of the prison population, the lack of social intercourse creates its own kind of punishment for someone whose community is already limited.

If you've ever had to endure quarantine for any reason, such as the pandemic of 2020–2021, the solitude might feel oppressive.

But if you practice it in small increments, along with silence, you'll find it a welcome relief from the noise and distraction of the outside world, no matter how welcome those distractions are.

The silence and solitude also hone your listening skills so that you more readily hear the voice of your Muse regardless of how softly she speaks.

Silence and solitude also heal you as a creative. Creativity is a challenge when you are stressed and overwhelmed. Like a cat whose fur has been rubbed the wrong way, silence and solitude smooth all that ruffled fur, those ragged nerves.

But you can't live and create only in silence. Some silences are not productive or helpful. The Prince, looking at the castle and its outbuildings, probably dumbfounded by all he sees, has to decide if this is a silence that needs breaking. Will he move forward or turn back?

Here is where you decide. Will you continue to keep your work isolated from the world? Will you create for yourself and your family, for the joy of it and to share that joy with a select few? Or do you want to move your work from your sheltered space into the more challenging environment of the world beyond the hedge? Do you want to break the silence around your work and creative dreams?

It is, of course, up to you. Any decision is right for you in this moment in time. Perhaps the Prince will come again if he is turned away at the door. Perhaps not. But the decision is yours.

If you are ready to break the silence, then the Prince is a welcome presence. In the early '90s, I applied to several craft shows in New York and Pennsylvania, curious to see what the response to my weaving would be. I enjoyed the interaction with people, as well as the exposure to many more craftspeople and their work. At one of those shows, one of the exhibitors, a jeweler, and I struck up a conversation. At one point, he suggested I apply to a big wholesale craft show that took place in Philadelphia and brought buyers from across the US and beyond. He felt my work qualified to be juried into the show.

He was, in that moment, the Prince, bringing the possibility of the world to my doorstep. Or my booth. If I heeded his suggestion, the relative safety and silence of my creative castle would be gone. My work—and I—would be exposed to the possibilities of criticism and rejection and more.

Remember the emcee for the Maui Writers Conference who stepped into my booth at another craft show? She, too, was the Prince, breaking the silence and safety of my castle walls.

You can't always rely, though, on someone else to be your prince. Sometimes you have to be the Prince for yourself. You have to break the silence, one way or another.

When I finally exhibited at that craft show the jeweler Prince recommended to me, I quickly realized that I couldn't stand and wait for someone to walk in or ask questions about my work. I had to engage potential customers. I had to be the Prince and break the silence if I wanted to make sales.

As you know, hours are spent creating the work. But as an exhibitor, I also spent time designing a booth and enticing display, creating handouts or brochures to inform the reader about the work and prices, and even packing up and driving to the show venue. Not selling anything feels like a curse cast at the christening. While I anxiously anticipated the first sale of the day, I had to talk, engage, promote. Once I had the first sale, the curse was broken. But I had to break the silence.

And this is where silence often wins out, because to break the silence and talk about our work is intimidating. Depending on where you are with the development of your work or how long you've been working at it, you may not be confident about it. Or, like me, you may have been taught as a child not to brag, so you hesitate to talk about the work, about the careful craftsmanship, the intricacy of the design, the richness of the colors. Convincing yourself that the work is good is challenge enough, but convincing someone else?

At one of my first craft shows, a couple walked into my booth. The wife was very taken by my one-sleeve shawl. They looked at the price, and the husband challenged me on it, wanting to know why the price was what it was. I tried to explain to him the uniqueness of the colorway, the fine finish to the fringe, and more. He was having none of it. "You can get something like this cheaper at Walmart," he said and stalked out of the booth with his kids and his wife, who smiled and shrugged an apology. I could have taken on his devaluation of my work, but I knew he wouldn't find anything else like it. Certainly not at discount store prices. I continued to make sales during the show. I refused to let his comments silence me.

You have to be ready to break the silence to defend yourself and your work.

YES, YOU HAVE TO MARKET

Over the years of doing craft shows, coaching creatives, and, now, coaching writers, I haven't run into too many creatives who like to do the marketing necessary to find the audience for their work or themselves. But if you don't break that silence, who will?

Decades ago, there was the myth of the discovered artist. Someone with position and discernment sees your work somewhere, somehow, and, determined to show you and the world what an artiste you are, searches you out, knocks on your door, and offers you the part, the exhibition, the contract that will make you a success.

There's a problem with that myth though. Aside from the fact that that seldom happens anymore, it misses the fact that for you to be discovered, your work had to be out there somewhere to begin with for the person to even know you and your art existed. They weren't searching through the woods looking for the quaint cottage where magic takes place.

They still aren't.

You have to break the silence. You have to find a way to connect your work to the world, to let the people out there, searching for just your type of magical gift, know that you have what they want. Not with braggadocio, waving the sword and telling people how you were the only one good enough and smart enough and brave enough to take on those thorns, but rather in a Pointer Sisters' "I'm so excited, I just can't hide it" kind of way.

You share the joy, the excitement, and a sense of discovery in your work with people. Is there some pride there? I hope so, for your sake, but only as part of your delight.

How you choose to share your work is up to you. With all of the technology available and some access to the internet, there is no excuse for not sharing your work or some sample of it. Social media, of course, is one way. Choose two or three platforms you feel comfortable using and participating in, and then do the work to create a presence. The keys to success and building an audience are consistency and building relationships. Don't post or share and then disappear for several months, only to show up again when you want to sell something. That's like the long-lost relative who calls or visits only when they need money for a new venture. Consider creating a calendar for your content and posts so you know ahead of time what you'll be posting when, and then it won't be such a challenge.

There are plenty of books out there on how to use social media, some specific to artists, writers, and other creatives. You'll find some listed in the resources section.

And if you can't just bring yourself to promote regularly, or if you don't have the time, then consider hiring someone who specializes in marketing and promotion for creatives or for people in your creative field. While working on this book, I hired an author assistant who helps with a newsletter and posting on social media, and she is worth every penny. I was able, because of her assistance, to develop a newsletter list and online presence while also ghostwriting, working on this book, and holding a bimonthly writers online retreat to work on novels. Although you may be used to doing everything yourself, you don't have to. And often, you shouldn't.

Social media isn't the only way to break the silence. Participate in professional conferences and send out letters or emails to gatekeepers in your field, such as gallery owners, agents, and more. Consider giving talks or leading workshops anywhere from your local library to online video classes to conferences.

It doesn't matter whether you are an introvert, a social introvert, or an extrovert; you can find a way to let others know about your work. Use your imagination for your marketing. You can be as creative with that as you are with your work.

Like the Prince, you know it's time to break the silence.

Journal Work

When was the last time you let yourself be silent and solitary, not as punishment but as renewal? Do you regularly schedule time for silence and solitude? If not, what would it feel like to give yourself that gift? What are any hesitations or fears around doing so? Conversely, what keeps you from breaking the silence about your work? Is it lack of knowledge or help? What can you do to change that? Is it fear of criticism of or lack of acceptance for your work? What steps can you take to get past them?

Ritual Work

This is a simple ritual. Make sure your phone is muted or, better yet, in another room. Don't turn on any music. Light a candle or anoint yourself with a calming essential oil such as lavender or chamomile or rose and then sit in a space of silence and solitude, breathing quietly. As you breathe, listen. What do you hear? The flame flickering? Sounds of nature? Sounds of the city? Listen to your breath as you breathe in and out. Drop your shoulders. Relax your belly. Can you hear your heart? How does it feel to be in silence? Sit for as long as feels comfortable. Repeat as often as possible, increasing the time by small increments.

Dreamwork

Sometimes you'll experience periods where it feels like your mind is working 24/7. When that happens, you need to sleep deeply and without being aware of or remembering your dreams. Put the date in your dream journal and ask the dream messengers to take the night off. Tell them that you'd like a night to sleep without remembering or being aware of dreams. I know it sounds strange, but it works.

PART FOUR

THE KISS

AWAKENING TO PASSION AND CREATIVE MANIFESTATION

The Prince saw that the whole of the court lay asleep, and up by the throne lay the King and Queen. Quiet was a presence in the castle, and only the breaths of the sleepers could be heard. The tread of his boot heels broke the silence and beat a rhythm as he strode from room to room, up one staircase after another. At last, he came to a door into a tower. He opened it and followed the winding stairs up and up. Could this be where the princess lay? Now he could hear his own breath and his heartbeat as well. At the top was another door. Of course he opened it.

There she lay, so still except for the rise and fall of her breasts. Now his pulse beat even faster. Here was the moment. Did he dare? But she was so beautiful. Her lips so tempting. He could not turn away, and he bent to kiss those tempting lips, finding them warm and sweet. They stirred beneath his, and when he raised his head he found that her eyes were open. She smiled up at him. "You are just as I dreamed you, sweet Prince."

The kiss. The marvelous, magical, transformative power of a kiss.

"Since the invention of the kiss, there have been five kisses that were rated the most passionate, the most pure. This one left them all behind." Grandpa reads to his sick-in-bed grandson in the movie *The Princess Bride*, also a fairy tale but a longer one.

The kiss between the Prince and Sleeping Beauty might not have been in the top five, but it is certainly memorable, as is the kiss the Prince gives Snow White. In both stories, the heroine is awakened by the kiss.

The kiss is where the magic lies, the magic that breaks the other magic of the curse, the spell of the thirteenth fairy.

But why a kiss? What is the magic in a kiss?

A kiss is a touch or press of the lips. Between sexual partners, an open-mouthed kiss will include tongues as well as lips. A kiss is given for many reasons, including love, affection, peace, greeting, sexual arousal or passion, respect, and friendship, and even as a symbolic gesture of devotion or surrender. There is an element of implied trust in a kiss, trust that no harm is intended.

A young woman in her early or teen years may imagine kissing or being kissed by another, and practice the act on her hand or a mirror to explore the experience and the sensations. Many remember their first kiss. Who gave it and when and where.

It's memorable because that kiss awakens you not only to the other but to yourself and the presence of your own attractive magic. A kiss also has the power to transform, as is seen throughout generations and numerous cultures of stories, including, of course, Beauty and the Beast.

Faith Hill captures the magic of that kiss in her song "This Kiss," when she sings, "It's that pivotal moment / It's unthinkable / This kiss, this kiss (unsinkable) / This kiss, this kiss . . " And if Briar Rose wanted to know if the Prince really loved her, then she'd follow the advice of Betty Everett in her song "His Kiss": "If you want to know, if he loves you so / It's in his kiss."

Okay. So, there's magic in a kiss, but what does that have to do with you and your creativity?

The kiss, especially in the songs and stories, usually implies an intimate . . . relationship. And isn't that what you want? Not with a prince or princess but with your creativity and your Muse. A relationship that grows and develops. A relationship that weathers the tests of time. A relationship that provides the opportunity to give birth and to nurture and care for the results of that. Which suggests that in your relationship with your creativity, you need trust, love, attraction, a willingness to change and compromise, a willingness to grow, a willingness to spend time both in the tower and in the world.

No matter which version you read of Sleeping Beauty, the kiss calls her back into the world, back into—as it is called in dream circles—waking reality, into the here and now, into engaging with a daily life that is measured and affected by time.

A real and seductive danger for a creative is to dream their creativity and life away. So many fascinating ideas and possibilities. So many what-ifs to explore a little bit here and a little bit there, but all within the safety of the dream or the tower.

People often use the term "ivory tower," especially when it comes to academia. The phrase means a place or state of privileged seclusion or separation from facts and the practicalities and necessities of the real world. But creatives also find themselves in an ivory tower, especially if they are fortunate enough to have support or be unfortunate enough to neglect their own well-being.

Just as Rapunzel must leave her tower, and Sleeping Beauty descend from hers, you as a creative cannot spend all your life imagining and dreaming up ideas without finally finishing and moving them out into the community, small or large.

And, of course, you need the rich material that life has to offer in order to keep dreaming new dreams and imagining new creative ideas.

You can imagine that Briar Rose and her prince didn't stop at one kiss. That the first kiss was followed by many more. And that's good. Especially if they were going to work toward their happily ever after. If you are going to move to your happily ever after, if you are going to brave the hedge, do the dreaming, create the work, market and promote the work . . .

You have to have a passion for the work.

Oh, not twenty-four hours a day, seven days a week. No. You don't find that passion operates 24/7 even among the most devoted of marriages. There are days and times when it feels like the work is drudgery, like the marketing and promotion is a pain in the . . well, uncomfortable as a thorny hedge. After bad reviews and rejection letters, and projects that won't cooperate no matter what, you will wonder why you should continue, and whether it is all worth it. That is when passion is important.

Remembering the thrill of a good review or many sales, the praise from a valued mentor or role model, or the creative project that succeeds beyond your vision for it will help you reexperience the passion of that first kiss.

But what is also needed is commitment—the wedding that ensures the happily ever after. In the Tarot, the card that shows up is the Four of Wands. Wands is the element of Fire (i.e., passion and will). Four represents stability. In many decks, you'll see a couple under a wedding canopy. When I do a reading for clients around their creativity, I tell them that this is the commitment card, the point at which to say, "I do," to your partner; in this case, your creativity or your Muse.

Because as the happy couple—or you and your Muse—will soon discover, the return to the world will be both joyful and challenging. To make it past the rough stages, the raising of kids, the concerns about income, dealing with the troublemakers who want to invade your realm, and the adventuring forth of one while the other tends the home fires, a commitment to each other and to the being that is the two of you together is necessary.

It's like building those strong stone walls around the castle to protect it and its inhabitants. Their purpose is security, not to keep people in or the world out. The gates open wide.

The commitment will help when the honeymoon stage is over. You know, when that initial excitement for the new project starts to wane and you start eyeing the other idea you had recently. Or when you have to meet deadlines, or fill orders, or show up for seemingly unending rehearsals. The stars in the eyes are gone, and now you face the reality. The commitment helps you stay with it, and when you stay with it, the relationship has an opportunity to deepen and grow. Or you discover it's not for you, after all. But you won't be certain about it if you don't commit and work at meeting the commitment to your creativity. Commitment is the fuel that keeps the creative fires, the passion and determination, burning.

That combination of passion and will is an important part of being a creative. It helps you do your work on a regular basis, like tending to a primary relationship.

Interestingly, according to the Eastern system of the chakras, the second chakra has special application to the kiss in the fairy tale.

The second chakra, located just below the belly button, and orange in color, is related to sexuality, pleasure, and . . . creativity. Not surprisingly, its location on the body is the area of the womb, so the connections among sexuality, pleasure, and creativity are important to consider in relation to the love, passion, and pleasure you bring to your creative work. What is also interesting is that this chakra is also related to self-worth, that idea mentioned in chapter 11. Making a commitment to your creativity means believing in the value, the worth, not just of the work but of you as the creator.

The kiss is not just the coming together of passion and creativity, but the joining of the receptive and proactive energies.

It's why I love this fairy tale as a metaphor for the creative life and process. As the old song says, you can't have one without the other. You can't lie around daydreaming or conscious dreaming or sleep dreaming of ideas and possibilities. Seeds never planted will wither and die.

You can't create and market without inspiration and vision; otherwise the blossom is without color and scent. The work stays on the surface and becomes mechanical instead of vital.

While this kiss of this fairy tale may not have made it into the top five kisses, it is a kiss that is passionate and promises life and creative abundance.

This kiss, this kiss . . .

Journal Work

Do you remember when you first fell in love with your creative work? Were you drawn to it because someone in your circle was doing it and you were curious, so they showed you how to do it? What was your first project? Do you still have it, or did you give it away? Do you remember the pride of accomplishment, or did it frustrate you? What about your experience with that first project made you start the second project?

Ritual Work

When you want to stir your creative fires and renew the passion for your work, try a simple ritual such as a cup of tea with cinnamon, or taking a hot bath with lit candles placed around you. Imagine your second chakra warming up and glowing with the passion and will to create in your medium. Feel it glow warmly and remind you of the "first kiss" of your creative work. Remind yourself that that passion, excitement, and enthusiasm are there for you to tap into when you are creating.

Dreamwork

Have you had dreams of celebrities or someone in your creative field that you admire? Did you find yourself being physically intimate with them in some way? It's not strange. It's rather common. I had a writer friend who once shared about having an experience of kissing Elvis Presley. After working through the dream with her, she realized that she wanted to integrate his sexuality, daring, and charisma in her own work. This is often the case with celebrity dreams. If you've had one, write down the qualities that you admire in this celebrity. Or qualities that you don't admire. What would you like to integrate or kiss hello? What would you like to get rid of or kiss goodbye?

HAPPILY EVER AFTER

They descended down the stairs from the tower together and discovered that not only had Briar Rose awakened but so had the entire court. The King and Queen gave great sighs, sat up, and looked around, astonished. The horses in the courtyard stood up and shook themselves and pranced about the courtyard. The dogs, too, jumped up and wagged their tails. The pigeons on the roof took their heads from under their wings and began cooing and then flew around the courtyard and out into the countryside. Even the fire in the kitchen flamed up, ready to cook the meat and boil the water. The cook, who had been waiting one hundred years to box the ears of the kitchen boy, did so, and the boy yelled, then proceeded to pluck the feathers from a fowl.

And the marriage of the offspring of two realms, the Prince and Princess, was celebrated with joy and splendor.

The descent from the upper levels back to ground level is an important movement, not just for the happy couple but for you as a creative as well. It's a movement from isolation and separation back into community and belonging. But it's not Briar Rose returning to family and friends by herself. Nor is the Prince descending on his own to retrace his steps back through the hedge to his horse.

The dreamer and the enactor work together, and so, in the marriage, two become one, a new entity that integrates the different aspects and gifts of the two.

Marriage is a ritual of commitment, as mentioned in chapter 10. Outside of the religious ceremonies in a temple or church, couples have, for centuries, found other ways to signify their union and make their commitment public. An African tradition that came to America with the slaves is jumping the broom together. The broom symbolizes the sweeping away of the past or evil, and stepping into a new life together. It's similar to carrying the bride over the threshold.

Another tradition that, like jumping the broom, is used in wedding ceremonies today is handfasting. This is a ceremony where the hands of the couple are joined together with the binding of a rope or ribbon or other binding. After the cord is wound around the clasped hands in a certain pattern, the ends of the cord are given to each member of the couple, who then pull on them, freeing their hands but leaving a knot in the middle of the cord, signifying the binding of their commitment, and leading to the phrase "tying the knot."

While some couples will elope or visit a government-approved official to perform a legally recognized ceremony, most couples makes their vows before witnesses, before their community. Why? Well, there is the pressure of having to live up to the public commitment, but in many ceremonies, there is a point where the witnesses or attendees are asked if they will support the couple and their commitment to each other. Their "I do" is a commitment of the community back to the couple.

In the ceremony, both the couple and the community make commitments and therefore are accountable.

The couple is accountable to the community to work at their commitment, to do the daily tending necessary for an enduring and healthy relationship. The community is accountable to supporting that couple, to provide backup when crises and discord arise, and to offer services to maintain the well-being of the marriage and, if any, offspring.

As a creative, the community of peers takes many forms—professional organizations, critique and accountability partners or groups, retreats, workshops and other learning opportunities, and access to information about trends, industry updates, and more.

You return their support by belonging, attending, learning, and creating.

Creativity, like love, does not grow and flourish in isolation.

And so the Prince and Briar Rose are married, and there is a great feast. The tale doesn't tell the reader whether any fairies were invited. After the last fiasco, you can imagine the King put a kibosh on that idea. Why invite—again—trouble?

The story has come almost full circle. Can Briar Rose's wish to have a child be far behind?

The movement of the couple from the tower to the lower levels of the castle applies to numerous aspects of the creative life.

After sleeping and dreaming for one hundred years, Sleeping Beauty must have hundreds of dreams waiting to be honored and given form in the waking, physical world, as you do. Only you won't have to struggle to remember them in order to use their inspiration, because you've dated, titled, and recorded them in your dream journal. Right? And the aspect of you that takes action on the dreams, the Prince, can start to write or paint or compose or do whatever with those inspirations and ideas.

Also think of the pairing as the marriage of dreamer/creator and the promoter/marketer. Because it's not enough to create the work. Those days are gone. You have to be willing to market and promote your work. And if it helps you get motivated to do that, think how excited the Prince and Sleeping Beauty were, racing down the steps of the tower to get to where they could share their joy and excitement with others. And how happy the royal family and all the other members of the court and the staff of the castle were to celebrate and share in their joy. You want to race down the steps of your creative tower and emerge from it in order to share not just the work but your joy and excitement about it.

Another aspect of the Prince's role in the partnership and the effort to share with the community is to seek representation from agents, editors, gallery owners, and others.

Please understand here that these aspects of the self, the dreamer and creator, or the dreamer/creator and the marketer/promoter, are defined as feminine or masculine roles because in the tale they are Prince and Princess. It's not about gender; it's about the activity as represented in the story. We are all dreamers and creators. We all need to be producers, marketers, and promoters. Or be willing to hire people who can fill those roles for us.

What I am proposing—yes, a pun—is that you commit to your Muse. And that that commitment is more than to love and honor; it is also to obey (i.e., to hear and then carry out). In other words, having received the inspiration, you commit to carrying it out, to making the idea real. And then you share it with the community, whether small or large.

A wedding is a commitment that the members of the couple give to each other. A wedding is also a commitment of the couple to the community, and the community to the couple. Unless you are going to forever hide your work in a drawer or a closet, you live your life in a community, and your creativity lives there with you.

And though you may not realize it, your creativity is a spark, a small flame that when combined with others' sparks creates light and hope in the world, just as the wedding of a couple does.

Think of all those "C" words—couple, community, commitment, celebration, and
. . .

Creativity.

All that when you say, "I do."

Journal Work

What does community mean to you? What creative communities do you belong to? Or have you stayed isolated, separate from the support and feedback of your peers?

What would you gain by being part of a community if you aren't yet? What is a downside to being part of a creative community? How might your work contribute to others?

Ritual Work

When was the last time you celebrated your creativity and its results with others? For this ritual work, invite a gathering of friends, not necessarily creative peers (although they can be), for a shared meal or hors d'oeuvres and beverages. Celebrate the beginning of a new work or the completion of one. Or share the challenges of your current project as a way to gather new energy and motivation. Toast them and toast the Muse.

Dreamwork

Incubate a dream, asking to talk with your Muse, and ask Her for what you need, either from her or from your community, in order to grow in your relationship. See what happens, who shows up. If, after a week or so, you don't remember a dream, try a conscious dream with the same intent. Be gentle around it. Don't force the process. And don't edit the dream information that comes to you. Live with the dream for a few days. And don't forget to record it in present tense.

THE END ... TO BEGIN AGAIN

And they all lived happily ever after.

The End.

Of course, happily ever after doesn't mean happy all the time. My husband and I have been married, at the time of writing this, for forty-seven years. And we are still living our happily ever after. But there has also been grief and anger and hurt and making up and worries and illnesses and deaths. So, no, not happy all the time.

As a creative, even one who listens to your Muse, who honors and acts on her inspirations and insights and who then shares the resulting work with your community, you know that you can live happily ever after with your Muse, but not happy all the time. If you are new to living and working with your Muse and haven't yet experienced the trials and tribulations of a committed relationship with your Muse, you will. Guaranteed.

Because it's the nature of all rewarding relationships. They don't last and endure because they're easy but because they aren't. While I don't believe that relationships have to be filled with angst and arguments, it is the nature of being human that we are going to disagree with each other over time. If you've been working in your creative medium for a while, you know that sometimes you may reach a point in your work where it feels like it's arguing with you. You disagree with it. You may get angry at it. Walk off and leave it alone for a while, until you can come back and engage with it from a new perspective.

If you are committed to a relationship, whether with an individual or with your work and the Muse, the challenges and conflicts cause you to grow individually and together because the challenges and conflicts lead to new understandings and even to a place of empathy and compassion.

As Ronny Cammareri says in the movie *Moonstruck*, "Love don't make things nice—it ruins everything. It breaks your heart. It makes things a mess. We aren't here to make things perfect. The snowflakes are perfect. The stars are perfect. Not us. Not us! We are here to ruin ourselves and to break our hearts and love the wrong people and *die*."

You could substitute creativity in that quote for love and have it sound just as true. Relationships, including your relationships with your work and the Muse, are messy and hard.

"...and die." Death. Not something you'd normally associate with love or creativity, but Ronny understands that nothing is forever. That everything comes to an end.

Remember the three Fates? Atropos is the Fate who cuts the life thread spun out and measured by Clotho and Lachesis, respectively. Of the three, she is the one who cannot be gainsaid, argued, or pleaded with. Even Zeus, the god of all the gods, cannot sway Atropos once she has decided to use her scissors and cut the thread of a life.

In my book *Weaving a Woman's Life: Spiritual Lessons from the Loom*, I share how I came to understand this lesson of Atropos's. As a weaver, when I had a warp on the loom it didn't matter where I was in the project—say, a shawl—I had to weave that shawl to the end and then cut it from the loom. Unlike sewing, I couldn't put down one project and pick up another to work on for a while. When working on the loom, I had to either finish the warp and cut it off, or cut the warp off before it was finished, wasting a lot of threads and yardage in order to wind and warp new threads onto the loom.

Only in the ending was a new beginning possible.

If you are one of those creatives who keep going back to a work to tweak and polish and refine it, not once but many times, then listen to Ronny. Nothing is perfect except snowflakes and stars, and there is just no sense in trying to compete with them. Or the perfect vision of your work that you have in your head. You have to let go. Put "The End" on your work and let it go.

You let it go so others can share in it and celebrate it—or reject it, because we are here, to paraphrase Ronny, to ruin ourselves and break our hearts and create the work imperfectly.

We do that in service and love to the work, ourselves, and the community.

You let go of the work so you can get started on the next project, which will, one hopes, exhibit some of the lessons learned from this one.

Moonstruck, in some ways, is a modern version of the Sleeping Beauty fairy tale. When the movie first opens, Loretta (Cher) is a bookkeeper doing accounts for a few local businesses, including her aunt and uncle's. Her hair, showing signs of gray, is pulled up into a twist or bun at the back of her head, and she wears a white blouse neatly tucked into a pencil skirt. She wears little makeup. After Johnny Cammareri (Ronny's brother) proposes to her and she accepts, she tells her mother that, no, she isn't in love with him. Loretta is living—if you can call it that—in an emotional tower, protecting herself from the pain of loss because of a previous experience. After meeting Johnny's brother, Ronny (I know, the names are confusing, but stay with me), they get into a heated, passionate argument, and he awakens her with his passion and . . . his kisses. After making love, and Loretta regrets it, Ronny begs her to go to the opera with him—just one date and then he won't bug her any more. She agrees, and because she is going to the opera, she decides to get her hair done. When she emerges from the salon, her hair is dark and loose around her shoulders. Her brows have been plucked and makeup applied. Next, she goes shopping for a dress and shoes. Emerging from the shop, a guy whistles at her. And when Ronny suddenly spies her at the opera house . . . well, you can imagine. Cinderella transformed. Sleeping Beauty awake. And the Prince is breathless.

Even the return to the castle and the feast that follows appear in the film. At the end, everyone, including Loretta's aunt and uncle and Johnny, are sharing a glass of champagne and toasting Ronny and Loretta's engagement and to *la famiglia*, the family.

And as the music starts and the credits roll, you imagine hearing, "And they lived happily ever after. The end."

Loretta is no longer asleep, and Ronny is no longer a lone wolf in his cave, another form of staying asleep.

It's important to finish projects. Never finishing is an attempt to continue to sleep and dream. It keeps you from risking the pain of rejection and criticism. As much as you'd like to protect your work and yourself from that exposure and pain, you can't. Atropos won't let you. For new ideas and projects to be born, old projects and ideas, one way or another, need to be cut off, need to end.

In the process, though, show compassion.

Compassion. That is something you don't need to have just for your work, but for yourself. Your relationship with your creativity requires it. Remember? You aren't here to be perfect. Or to create perfectly.

That means you don't beat yourself up when a creative project doesn't measure up to the vision you had for it. You don't kick yourself because you should be producing more, better, or more consistently, or whatever else you tend you harangue yourself about.

Love the process of growing and developing as an artist, because it is a process.

You wouldn't expect to get out of bed tomorrow and run a marathon (unless, of course, you've run them before), so don't expect to get "it" right the first time out or even the tenth time out.

Love the work with all its foibles and let it go. Let it go so you can begin again.
So you can start a new story, a new "Once upon a time."
The End. Once upon a Time. The End. Once upon a Time.
One implies the other. Get comfortable with both.
And keep enchanting creativity.

Journal Work

What does "The End" look like in your work? The final stitch? The last rub of polish on a surface? The final line of dialogue before the curtain? How do you feel when you reach "The End"? Do you give yourself time to recover and to celebrate your achievement? Have you learned anything from this project that you can apply to the next one?

Ritual Work

Find a thread, strand of yarn, or piece of string. If you can, choose a color that you feel reflects your work; it might be green because the project spoke of growth or the earth, for instance. Or pink to represent the feminine or sweetness or innocent love. Find a pair of scissors or shears.

Open the ritual by lighting a candle or taking several deep breaths or something else that you like to do. Think about the work you've completed. The measuring out you did of words or notes or yards or something else. Pull that thread or yarn to a length that feels representative of the work, and then, at the same time, cut the thread and say, "The End." Feel the ending. The letting-go of the work. Take a deep breath. Release. And close the ritual. You can leave the yarn or thread wound and on your creativity altar. Or keep it for a few days and then burn it or bury it to release it back to the earth. Or store in a small box or envelope as a reminder.

Dreamwork

At the next new moon, ask for a dream of new beginnings. Dreams are usually active around the new and full moons. Try to record as many as you can remember. Note what you may be releasing, and what may be waiting for you to claim. New messages from your Muse appear shortly after the new moon. Date, title, and record.

EPILOGUE

With a satisfied sigh, the book closes. The story is over, and it is time to return to the "real" world.

Or is it? One thing I think creatives do well is straddle the threshold between this realm and the imaginal one. Maybe that's why, when I teach dreamwork to writers and other creatives, they seldom have trouble dropping into conscious dreaming. Creatives are often halfway there to begin with.

The challenge is more often one of staying in the waking or real world when necessary than it is to access the other world, the place of imagination, fairy tales, and dreams.

The tools and exercises shared in this book will help you move back and forth across the threshold more easily and productively.

And being able to move from one realm to the other more easily means you don't have to worry about getting stuck or being unable to get back, even when you are stressed, exhausted, ill, or dealing with crises.

You are the protagonist of your creative story, both Prince and Sleeping Beauty. You are the one with the power to dream, to face the hedge of thorns and the walls of silence and to brave the unknown. You are the one to descend back into the world with the gifts of your imagination.

You are both "Once upon a time" and "The End," and, with these tools and your creativity . . . You have the power to create your happily ever after.

BOOKS

Creativity & Other

Cameron, Julia. *The Artist's Way: A Spiritual Path to Higher Creativity*. New York: Jeremy P. Tarcher / Perigee Books, 1992.

Mountain Dreamer, Oriah. *What We Ache For: Creativity and the Unfolding of Your Soul*. San Francisco: HarperSanFrancisco, 2005.

Pressfield, Stephen. *The War of Art: Break Through the Blocks and Win Your Inner Creative Battles*. New York: Grand Central, 2002.

Scardamalia, Paula Chaffee. *Weaving a Woman's Life: Spiritual Lessons from the Loom*. Rensselaerville, NY: Nettles & Green Threads, 2006.

Syme, Becca. *Dear Writer, You Need to Quit: What to Keep, What to Quit, What to Question*. QuitBooks for Writers Book 1. Bozeman, MT: Hummingbird Books, 2019.

Fairy Tales

Andersen, Hans Christian. *Hans Christian Andersen: The Complete Fairy Tales and Stories*. Foreword by Virginia Haviland. Translated by Erik Christian Haugaard. Anchor Folktale Library. New York: Anchor Books, 1983.

Calvino, Italo. *Italian Folktales: Selected and Retold by Italo Calvino*. New York: Houghton Mifflin Harcourt, 1980.

Perrault, Charles. *The Complete Fairy Tales*. Translated and introduced by Christopher Betts. Oxford World's Classics Hardbacks. Oxford: Oxford University Press, 2009.

Pullman, Philip. *Fairy Tales from the Brothers Grimm: A New English Version*. New York: Viking Penguin, 2012.

Warner, Marina. *From the Beast to the Blonde: On Fairy Tales and Their Tellers*. New York: First Noonday, 1996.

Dreamwork

Delaney, Gayle. *All about Dreams.* San Francisco: HarperSanFrancisco, 1998.

Epel, Naomi. *Writers Dreaming.* New York: Carol Southern Books, 1993.

Jung, Carl G., M.-L. von Franz, Joseph L. Henderson, Jolande Jacobi, and Aniela Jaffe. *Man and His Symbols.* London: Aldus Books, 1964.

Moss, Robert. *Conscious Dreaming.* New York: Crown Trade Paperbacks, 1996.

Moss, Robert. *The Secret History of Dreaming.* San Francisco: New World Library, 2008.

Moss, Robert. *The Three Only Things: Tapping the Power of Dreams, Coincidence & Imagination.* San Francisco: New World Library, 2007.

RITUALS & JOURNALS

Baldwin, Christina. *Life's Companion: Journal Writing as a Spiritual Quest.* New York: Bantam Books, 1990.

Biziou, Barbara. *The Joy of Ritual: Spiritual Recipes to Celebrate Milestones, Ease Transitions, and Make Every Day Sacred.* New York: Cosimo Books, 2006.

Hinchman, Hannah. *A Life in Hand: Creating the Illuminated Journal.* Salt Lake City, UT: Peregrine Smith Books, 1991.

Tarot

Pollack, Rachel. *Tarot Wisdom: Spiritual Teachings & Deeper Meanings.* Woodbury, MN: Llewellyn, 2008.

Scardamalia, Paula Chaffee. *Tarot for the Fiction Writer: How 78 Cards Can Take You from Idea to Publication.* Atglen, PA: Schiffer, 2019.

MUSIC & RECORDINGS

Gordon, David, and Steve Gordon. *Drum Medicine.* CD. Topanga, CA: Sequoia Records, 1999.

Moss, Robert. *Dream Gates.* Audiobook on CD. Boulder, CO: Sounds True, 1997.

Scardamalia, Paula Chaffee. *The Tower in the Woods: Dreaming Your Creativity Awake.* CD. 2004.

Sondheim, Stephen, and James Lapine. *Into the Woods.* CD. New York: Masterworks Broadway, 1988.

FILMS

Daldry, Stephen, dir. *Billy Elliott*. DVD. Universal City, CA: Universal Home Video, 2000. British dance drama film written by Lee Hall.

Jewison, Norman, dir. *Moonstruck*. DVD. Santa Monica, CA: MGM/UA, 1987. American romantic comedy film written by John Patrick Shanley and starring Cher, Nicolas Cage, Danny Aiello, Olympia Dukakis, and Vincent Gardenia.

Reiner, Rob, dir. *Princess Bride*. DVD. Beverly Hills, CA: MGM, 1987. American fantasy adventure comedy film starring Cary Elwes, Robin Wright, Mandy Patinkin, Chris Sarandon, Wallace Shawn, André the Giant, and Christopher Guest.

MATERIALS & SUPPLIES

Oils

Artisan Aromatics. www.artisanaromatics.com. Pure aromatherapy, essential oils, and products since 1993.

Garden of One. www.gardenofone.com. Energetic preparations and tools to transform.

Rocky Mountain Oils. www.rockymountainoils.com. A leading purveyor of 100% pure, natural, and authentic essential oils, expertly crafted blends, and nutritional products, since 2004.

Journals

Moleskine. https://moleskine.com. Journals and other objects that inspire imaginations and fuel creative practice, a platform that celebrates talent, champions originality, and cherishes long-term thinking.

Paperblanks. www.paperblanks.com. Beautiful journals that are objects of art and creativity that, in turn, inspire creativity, empower expression, and celebrate special moments.

Zequenz. www.zequenz.com. The ultimate masterpiece roll-up journal, with numerous colors, three sizes, and different inside pages.

Pen Boutique. www.penboutique.com. Both from their Maryland store and online, they sell a range of writing instruments—fountain pens, ballpoint pens, and more—in a range of prices, along with inks and other accessories.

WEBSITES & LINKS

Ciro Marchetti. www.ciromarchetti.com. His beautiful illustrations and artwork are available in numerous Tarot decks, Lenormand decks, a Kipper deck, silk spread cloths, and more. His images are also found on puzzles located on other sites such as Amazon.

Coworking Resources. www.coworkingresources.org. A publication that aims to provide the most comprehensive, unbiased guides for coworking-space owners to run a more efficient space.

Divining the Muse. www.diviningthemuse.com. Book coaching and creativity consults using dreamwork, Tarot, and rituals.

Moon River Rituals. www.moonriverrituals.com. Resources including podcasts on rituals for weddings, baby blessings, funerals, memorials, seasonal cycles, and daily magic.

TED Talk by Elizabeth Gilbert. https://www.youtube.com/watch?v=4HBJa279i8M.

Paula Chaffee Scardamalia is a book coach, a dream and Tarot intuitive, and the author of *In the Land of the Vultures* (novel) and *Tarot for the Fiction Writer*. For 20 years, Paula's presented workshops across the country at national and regional Romance Writers of America conferences and meetings, the San Diego University Writers Conference, and the International Women's Writing Guild. Since 2009, Paula has published *Divine Muse-ings*, a weekly e-newsletter on writing, creativity, dreams, and Tarot. She was dream consultant for *PEOPLE Country Magazine* and is the award-winning author of *Weaving a Woman's Life: Spiritual Lessons from the Loom.*